TIMIDITY
HOW TO OVERCOME IT

THE TEN TITLES IN THE

MENTAL EFFICIENCY SERIES

∽

∽

FUNK & WAGNALLS COMPANY
Publishers
NEW YORK AND LONDON

MENTAL EFFICIENCY SERIES

TIMIDITY
HOW TO OVERCOME IT

By YORITOMO-TASHI

WITH COMMENTS BY B. DANGENNES

AUTHORIZED EDITION

TRANSLATED BY MARY W. ARTOIS

FUNK & WAGNALLS COMPANY
NEW YORK   LONDON
1916

ANNOUNCEMENT

The purpose of this book is explained by its title—"Timidity: How to Overcome It." It has been crystallized in the maxim, "Let us not close the door of Life to any human being by refusing him its key—the recognition of his worth."

There are some folks in this great world of ours who commend Timidity as a virtue to be encouraged rather than a fault to be decried. These people consider all assertiveness as arrogance. To them the man or the woman that pushes to the front deserves to be sent to the rear. It is fortunate that this is not the popular view. The world smiles on the impudence of some men, while it glories in the dare and the dash of others.

In the teachings of Yoritomo-Tashi, the famous Japanese philosopher, included in the twelve lessons, which are presented and explained with care by Mr. B. Dangennes, in the following pages, the reader is told at the outset that Timidity is a mistaken virtue; a weakness that leads to the mistrust of self and which causes fear of ridicule. Those who think less of what the world, or others, think of them, and more of the matter in hand or purpose in view, will overcome that spirit of diffidence to which they may trace all their lost opportunities.

Timidity is a disease which affects the mind. In the face of danger, it roots some to the spot, while it gives wings to the heels of others. It is the aim of this Japanese philosopher to teach the reader how to check the growth of this disease and finally to eradicate it.

The timid man is not qualified to hold important office; he lacks the nerve that would shoulder responsibility, and is happy only when the necessity for taking the initiative passes him by. Timidity procrastinates; it puts off until to-morrow what it could do to-day; its foster-sister is indecision. Sensitive to the dangers that it may encounter, it is beaten almost before it has determined to strike. Such is the temperament before which the doors of opportunity are constantly closing.

Yoritomo-Tashi compares Timidity with over-confidence and daring, and, considering it in its many phases, demonstrates how it may prove an enemy to progress and business success, for it destroys confidence in self, leads to hesitancy in speech and manner, and causes that despondency which breaks the spirit and finally yields to despair.

To those who suffer from Timidity and wish to overcome it, the Japanese sage comes with words of encouragement. Let them follow his teachings and soon they will find that the diffidence from which they have been suffering has vanished; that they have overcome Timidity and become possest of that dignity by which the dauntless and intrepid command the respect which leads to success in life.

THE PUBLISHERS.

PREFACE

THE theories of the eminent Japanese philosopher Yoritomo-Tashi have resulted in the formation of another school of philosophy. Therefore, it is with the greatest pleasure that I undertake to comment on the maxims of this philosopher, while applying them to modern life

Yoritomo-Tashi expresses himself in a direct style, and he has a deep insight into the human soul, which enables him to define its various states. He possesses also this advantage over many other philosophers—he is not prosy, nor depressing. His teachings are illustrated by parables in which the poetry of the Far East stands out in vivid coloring, like a Japanese print.

Yoritomo-Tashi is superior to many thinkers in the fact that he is not satisfied with merely pointing out an evil; he analyzes its causes, and, in regard to mental defects, he indicates the cure.

I derived great pleasure from my first visit to the little provincial museum in which Yoritomo-Tashi's wonderful manuscripts re-

pose. And this pleasure was renewed a year
later. As in the tale of "The Sleeping Beauty
in the Woods," the custodian of this museum
seemed to have been asleep ever since the day
I called. He was surrounded by stuffed animals posed in attitudes suggesting their habits,
and he looked scarcely more alive than they.
The loud-ticking clock at one end of the room
was the only sign of life in this abode of silence
and oblivion.

It was with a feeling of awe that I entered
the small manuscript room, where, if it had not
been for the vigilance of the custodian's wife,
I could have traced the footprints I had made
on my previous visit, for no one had been there
to efface them since the preceding year. At
least this is what the good man told me, as he
turned pages covered with the writings of my
friend, Commander B——, who had translated
Yoritomo's philosophy.

In my memory there still lingered the remembrance of the advice, the precepts, the
deductions, and the symbols which I now re-
joiced to see again, and I was amazed at his
psychological mind, which was able to treat so
many different subjects, in turn, in such a
masterly manner. And, as when standing be-

fore a display of precious jewels, each of equal value, but of every conceivable form, we hesitate, so captivated with each one as we see it that we can not tell which one to admire the most, so I pondered a long while before making up my mind to what part of his writings I should devote my especial attention.

For Yoritomo is one of those learned men who do not confine themselves to specializing on certain disorders. As a philosopher, he made wide researches in all branches while lauding the virtues especially necessary to attain that wisdom which is one of the most advantageous forms of Harmony, from which all Happiness flows.

What are we striving for in this life if not to attain happiness, which each one of us views from a different aspect?

There are, however, certain rules that must be observed in order to reach this enviable state. There are also certain dangers that must be avoided. In fact, we must overcome and eradicate our faults as energetically as we would rid ourselves of an enemy.

Among these faults, says Yoritomo, is "Timidity," which many narrow-minded men wrongly treat so indulgently that they come to view as commendable a quality which they should most vigorously condemn.

So in our age of rapid evolution and strenuous competition, it seems to me a matter of intense interest to present here the precepts and the teachings which the renowned Yoritomo left us so many centuries ago, the great power and truth of which Time has not only confirmed, but magnificently maintained.

B. Dangennes.

CONTENTS

LESSON I

A MISTAKEN VIRTUE

"MANY educators," says Yoritomo-Tashi, "make the great mistake of extolling modesty, and condoning timidity.

"This mistaken virtue, even when accompanied by substantial qualities, will always be an obstacle in the path leading to the Best, the goal for which we all should aim.

"Mistrust of ourselves, the source of timidity, always springs from lack of confidence in our own strength, and must weaken us by hindering us from giving to our thoughts and their realization the inspiration necessary to exalt them."

There are a thousand forms of timidity, some quite natural, in a way physical; others—the most usual—originating from a mental state, which we are too weak to overcome.

"Timidity," says the venerable Nippon, "usually traces its origin to many sentiments, which are but rarely elevating.

13

"The loss or weakening of the will-power is the principal cause of these attacks of timidity.

"Excessive self-esteem is another cause.

"The fear of displeasing, or of not appearing as brilliant as we would like.

"The feeling of awkwardness, that increases under the gaze of strangers.

"Lacking the energy to concentrate, thereby causing one's thoughts to become confused, so that they can not be marshaled at will.

"Indolence in practising developing the 'Idea,' but slowly formed, which we know we can formulate only when too late.

"The difficulty we find in analyzing our thoughts, which results in our not knowing exactly what we want.

"And, above all, the certainty which one feels most keenly, that words too slowly strung together, but imperfectly interpret a thought which the speaker was unable to express clearly."

"There is," says Yoritomo, further on, "another form of timidity called awkwardness, which is usually caused by a person having an exaggerated idea of his own importance, causing him to imagine that every eye is fixt upon him."

The timid person is very sensitive. An incident which other people would not notice, affects him most keenly.

An apparent coldness, a look which he considers unsympathetic wounds him, especially as his defect isolates him, and causes him to develop great perspicacity.

But, as these observations are based on appearances, rather than facts, and as these conclusions are founded on details that have been disputed for a long time, often starting from a false premise, the timid person brings upon himself much unnecessary suffering, the disclosure of which would greatly surprize persons blest with good reasoning powers.

"Timidity," says the philosopher, "may be compared to a magnifying-glass which accentuates and magnifies the most minute forms a hundredfold, but includes so small a space that we can see only a little portion of the object."

It can not be denied that timidity destroys all ability, when it annihilates the will.

"Those who are afraid of being laughed at, suffer the most.

"This is, moreover, one of the least interesting kinds of timidity," says Yoritomo, "for it springs from an exaggerated self-esteem

III.1

and the fear of not appearing sufficiently brilliant.

"This fear, in timid persons, whose minds never retain an idea long enough to mature it, nearly always occasions a distressing stammering, and contributes still more to increase their trouble.

"When in this state, their self-love—violently at variance with their feeling of inferiority—blinds them, and so they are put out of countenance, and do all the awkward things they dreaded, thereby making themselves perfectly ridiculous."

"I had," adds the venerable Shogun, "a young neighbor whose father was in a position which gave him access to the most brilliant assemblies.

"At these gatherings he became noted for his awkwardness, and his maladroitness.

"If offered a cup of tea he would take hold of it in such a way as to spill the contents on his clothing, and this incident would plunge him into still deeper confusion.

"At meals he would handle his chop-sticks so clumsily as to obtain only a few grains of rice, his bowl remaining three-quarters full a long while after every one else had emptied his.

"If he was obliged to salute any one, he would advance blushing, hesitating, apparently seeing nothing round him, striking against objects that came across his path, stumbling in the interstices of the matting; in fact, appearing at the very greatest disadvantage.

"His father having heard that, in addition to commanding armies, I had devoted myself to the study of mental disorders, hunted me up one day and asked me if I would have the kindness to interest myself in his son, and try to cure him—for this excessive timidity had become an unbearable burden to them both.

"Through the bamboo hedges that separated our two gardens I had often perceived the young man, and been struck with the freedom of his movements, in contrast to his habitual embarrassment.

"Therefore, I immediately came to the conclusion that as his awkwardness only manifested itself in public, he must belong to that class of timid persons which might certainly be called conceited, for the principal cause of their embarrassment and their affectation lies in the conviction that they fasten the attention of others on themselves to such a degree that every one notices their slightest gesture.

"So I took what I considered the best means of convincing myself of this fact.

" 'This is your son?' said I, to his father.

" 'But you are already acquainted with him!'

" 'I must confess that I had not noticed him.'

" 'Alas, can this be true. You were certainly at the house of our friend, Samourai Long-Ho, yesterday, and you must have seen what a ridiculous figure he cut.'

" 'How?'

" 'Don't you remember? Just as he was making his grand salute on being presented, he stammered, turned round as tho trying to make his escape, became entangled in the folds of a rug, and, to save himself from falling, caught hold of a table filled with china. . . . The table upset, making a great clatter, while my unhappy boy fled in confusion.'

" 'Really,' said I, in an absent-minded manner. 'I remember this little incident, but I think you attach too much importance to it, for my friend and I were so engrossed in an interesting discussion that we paid but little attention to it, or to the person who caused it.'

"Immediately the young man's countenance brightened. I was glad to note that I had not wrongly classified him; he certainly belonged to the group of timid persons in which I had placed him.

"In the first place, I made him conceal his identity by introducing him in company as an obscure pupil of mine. Thus, feeling that his identity was unknown, he gradually lost his exaggerated sense of responsibility.

"Reassured by the thought that obscure clerks would never be able to attain the distinction of a *daimio* (noble) such as he, he gradually gained an ease of manner when among people, for he felt convinced that the humble student he was personating would pass unnoticed among the philosophers by whom we were usually surrounded, and after a few months he regained his composure, which the sight of people had formerly caused him to lose. In fact, I succeeded so well that, when I returned him to his father, he was proof against that absurd self-conceit which, by convincing him that he was the sinecure of all eyes, had caused him to behave in a vacillating manner, and had disconcerted him."

The only kind of timidity that Yoritomo tolerated was what he called "Excessive mistrust of oneself."

He defined it as follows:

"This is the only kind of timidity that does not spring from the clash of deleterious influences.

"It is, however, just as much of a defect, as it weakens one's energy, tho its starting-point is exempt from evil.

"To this class belong persons who are conscious of being ugly or infirm; those who underestimate their own worth, and lack the energy necessary to conquer their fault; in a word, all those who feel themselves inferior—with or without cause—in the presence of others, and lack the will-power indispensable to modify this condition.

"Rarely, however, do the timid warrant our taking an interest in them. Disgraced or incompetent persons scarcely ever endure their lot uncomplainingly. This mistaken virtue, called timidity, soon degenerates into open antipathy toward everybody who offends them."

In his matter-of-fact way, he good-naturedly remarks:

"The timid who escape this pitfall, those who live all their lives long without hating their superiors, are the *élite*, I may say the elect. But these must not be cited as examples; for the march toward the 'Best,' which should be the main object of all progress, especially requires men of executive ability.

"Other timid persons, feeling that they are cut off from sympathy, shrink within themselves until they feel like outsiders in the midst of company.

"But this kind of timidity rarely preserves its original purity. The person so afflicted soon cultivates solitude, and secretly thinks himself superior to others, to which cause he attributes the fact that other people stand aloof from him.

"The best proof of this tendency is that the embarrassment disappears when the afflicted person finds himself face to face with those who are not his equals.

"When with his inferiors, he behaves naturally, even affably, and when with his superiors, his extreme awkwardness causes him to resort to a praiseworthy reserve."

These very sensible remarks hold good to all time.

A further proof that timidity is a real defect —no matter what causes it—is, as in the case under discussion, that the premises produce illogical deductions.

It is not rational that intellectual equality should be a check to sympathy.

We see, however, that the timid affiliate more readily with those of a different status.

Therefore, the timid person, through "mistrust in himself," becomes abnormal as well, for sympathy, which makes people effusive—an emotion diametrically opposite to timidity—is shown by him under circumstances in which people with well-balanced minds would have hesitated to express themselves.

"Excessive fear of public opinion is also a frequent source of timidity," says the venerable Japanese, who illustrates this maxim by the following anecdote:

"One day we were holding a great council arguing a much-disputed diplomatic question.

"Our partizans were especially afraid of one of our adversaries, Long-Shu, a man of great ability, but afflicted with timidity.

"We were especially alarmed when he began to speak. But just at this moment the man nearest him whispered in his ear that a detail of his toilet was disarranged.

"This caused his defeat.

"Long-Shu immediately became embarrassed; the fear of ridicule—so strong in all timid persons—overcame him, and he stammered. Now the smiles which he thought he detected in the eyes of the audience, completed his discomfiture, and he left the place, after having spoken a few sentences, in great embarrassment; thus deserting a cause which, perhaps, he might have gained, if the excessive fear of public opinion had not caused him to magnify into a fault a thing which might have remained unnoticed. In fact, many of us accused his neighbor of causing his embarrassment.

"Timidity is nearly always the result of a confused state of mind, for it often springs from the doubt felt regarding the sympathy one craves.

"Nevertheless, the timid person is afraid of those who are demonstrative; when approached by them, he evades them, at the same time he suffers because he can not overcome the embarrassment which hinders this familiarity.

"He secretly desires it, but is not able to make up his mind to face the physical effort which even the consciousness of the effort would cause him to feel.

"What causes this difficulty, if not the thwarting of one's wishes by the conviction of not being able to make the effort to bring them about?"

A few pages further on we find a very interesting anecdote, in which Yoritomo draws a graphic simile regarding the state of mind of a timid person.

"There was," says he, "a man who became a very skilful painter. He excelled every one in painting large birds in flight, on thin paper, and no one was more skilful than he in painting plants so that they seemed to float on the dark waters, like faces of the drowned with the light shining on them.

"One day he tried to paint a figure that would strike the beholder with terror, for he wanted to use it in illustrating a book on the history of magic.

"He began by sketching one of those frightful heads seen in the most horrible nightmares, then he endowed his figure with terrible attributes.

"Some days later, on entering his house as night was falling, he was frozen stiff with fright on seeing the chimera he had created, and, altho he did all he could to overcome this feeling, it increased until the day he had the picture removed from his house.

"The timid person is just like this man.

"He exaggerates, and gives great weight to causes of anxiety which originate solely in his imagination; in a smile he sees irony; in impassibility, contempt.

"In every gesture another person makes he thinks he perceives unfavorable criticism. He fears praise as much as criticism, and suffering extremely from the one, he fears the other, which, by forcing him to make a reply, puts him in a pitiable plight.

"One of the torments of the timid is apprehension. It is the constant apprehension of feeling himself to be inferior, and of inviting ridicule; and, as the least thing frightens him, he finally takes refuge in solitude, thereby avoiding coming in contact with any outside influences."

"One of the principal afflictions of the timid," says Yoritomo, "is blushing. The most trifling incident suffices, at all times, to spread a blush over their faces, thus marking them for the attention they fear.

"The timorous spirit of the timid person— making him subservient to the opinions of others—readily causes him to fear that an unfavorable comparison may be made between the subject of the conversation at the moment, and the blushing which came when least expected.

"If the subject under discussion be a person,

the obsession becomes still stronger, and, when augmented by fear, it is impossible for the timid to hear the name of this person mentioned without feeling hot waves, accompanied by high color, mount to their faces.

"And the memory of the agony experienced only increases this propensity, which occurs so often as to become a real nuisance.

"The more so because timidity is always accompanied by exceedingly delicate sensations, the fruit of constant self-analysis when in mental solitude.

"This power of concentration, usually so valuable, is fatal to the timid, for it leaves them struggling with their chimera, thereby redoubling their torture.

"It tends to disconcert them, especially as they foresee the hostility, or the indifference, of others more accurately than people gifted with a well-balanced mind.

"Furthermore, we have seen that they quickly imagine this indifference to be hostility, and this hostility to be persecution."

From these facts we conclude that Yoritomo speaks the truth when he says that excessive modesty is a mistaken virtue, as it springs from vanity, egotism, and lack of energy.

According to his teaching, we have written, in a preceding book, the following sentence, which can not be repeated too often:

"Energy is the highest goal of all things, and the world belongs to the energetic."

LESSON II

HOW TO PREVENT THE GROWTH OF TIMIDITY

"WHEN I was one of the fervent disciples of Lang-Ho, the celebrated mind specialist, my master," says Yoritomo, "took me with him to the country one day.

"We walked through a magnificent garden in which a celebrated arboriculturist was busy exercising his skill in planting and cultivating trees, the fine fruit of which was to be reserved for the table of the Son of Heaven, who rules over the Middle Empire.

"Everything in the garden was arranged to charm the eye and the sense of smell, and calculated to make one envious.

"There were large trees, with branches so heavily laden with fruit that they nearly touched the ground; there were other trees, like the globe-flower, with their golden balls clustered all along the branches; and others still, surrounded by foliage, sparkled like uncut jewels.

28

"I never became tired of admiring them, and Lang-Ho listened complaisantly to my remarks.

"Then he led me into another orchard where the skill of man had done but little in the way of cultivation. Here branches shot out in every direction, bearing fruit that was partly hidden by thick boughs.

" 'See, my son,' said the master, 'these two gardens represent life: in the first the fruit, being carefully cultivated, exposed in such a way as to ensure its best development, and cleared of leaves which would keep off the sunlight, ripens and grows to perfection, just as man should do when his narrow prejudices have been eradicated by long culture, and his opinions rendered valuable by giving them the orientation that his mind demands.

" 'But in this orchard, where everything is left to the care of nature, only the fruit that has sufficient energy to disengage itself from its leafy prison is likely to survive and be palatable. Some specimens are very fine, but all the fruit which has not had sufficient strength to push through the foliage that sheltered it will remain stunted and colorless; much of it will become cracked, and a great part of the remainder will rot on the stem without even having made an attempt to reach the light and the warm sunshine.

" 'This is the fate reserved for the timid. They pass their lives retired within themselves, far distant from beautiful harmony, the creator of happiness.

" 'O my son!' he added, 'as it is your vocation to be a spiritual leader, as well as a warrior, remember this lesson, and reflect that timidity may annihilate the most precious gifts. It prevents one's talents from breaking down the fortress of bashfulness which surrounds them, just as this foliage conceals and stifles some of the fruit we see here.' "

As I remarked in the preface of this book, Yoritomo was not content with merely pointing out the evil, and giving a minute description of its causes, for his chief concern was to find the cure.

In a preceding chapter we read how he applied his theory to a case of timidity, discovered its origin, and the means of conquering and expelling the enemy.

But his dream was vaster still.

"To care for people afflicted with mental disorders," says he, "is well, but to prevent these disorders is better."

And being very fond of parables, he adds:

"It is certainly good to straighten up a plant that the wind has bent, but it would have been better to have thwarted this inclination by placing it in a more sheltered location, or in providing it, from the first, with a prop which would have permitted it to shoot up straight and supple, with no inclination to deviate."

"Timidity," adds he, "is rarely natural. It is only noticed in children when an injudicious education has made them intractable, and mistrustful of their own worth.

"Do animals which have had no experience in coming in contact with man, fear his approach?

"They only become frightened and wild when experience has demonstrated to them that these men chase them, surprize them, and destroy them.

"A child, likewise, is not born timid."

We have stated in a volume, entitled "La Volunté" (The Will), how very necessary it is to sow seeds in the heart of the child, from the very first months of his life, even before he is able to unravel the chaos of his sensations and exterior impressions.

According to the doctrine of the Shogun, this
III.2

might almost apply to the subject of timidity.

He thinks that educators play a most important part, and that it is their task to prevent the growth of this defect.

"From the most tender age, it is good," says he, "to let the child feel that he has responsibilities and to inculcate in him a pride in his personality.

"Of course, he must not be permitted to feel that he is better than others, for that might lead to his becoming very vain.

"On the contrary, he must know how to identify himself with things around him, and be taught how to look at them.

"If it be absolutely necessary to guide him in his decisions, childish tho they be, it would be injudicious to dictate them to him. The child should, when very young, be taught to govern himself, without relying exclusively on the advice of his superiors.

"Most of the naturally timid are so in consequence of having formed the habit of making no decision without the guidance of another's will. But if excessive solicitude produced unfavorable results, severity sometimes attains the same undesirable end.

"A child who trembles before his parents and

professors, commences life under very unfavorable conditions. The fear of being reprimanded, which he can not always avoid, makes him restless and suspicious. By repeatedly hearing fault found with everything he does, he comes to mistrust himself. This severity, the cause of which he but imperfectly understands, at last seems to him to be without any motive, and if he does not rebel he is sure to become a victim of timidity, which is prejudicial to all effort toward the 'Best.'

"If children were encouraged to be more confidential" says Yoritomo, "timidity would tend to disappear."

In fact, what one should especially dread in the child is the inclination to retire within himself, and to avoid expressing his thoughts, for fear of not being understood.

"It is very wrong," he tells us, "not to appear to consider as serious the childish questions that the little one asks on every occasion.

"By not replying to them, or by doing so in an offhand way, we make them conscious of the weakness of their intellect, and their lack of importance from a moral standpoint.

"We must not be astonished that some timorous natures feel themselves of so little consequence that they mistrust themselves, and, starting from that point, become incapable of taking the initiative in anything.

"It is very necessary, on the contrary, to study children, so that they will not notice the difference of age, so that the hierarchy will seem to them but a kind of protection, something that will sustain them, and promote a trust and confidence which will be rewarded with advice, instead of reprimands.

"The buds open gradually to the warmth of the spring, but close up and dry when touched by icy winds, or the burning heat of summer."

One excellent way of preventing the formation and development of timidity in the young is to allow them great latitude, and to let them learn to assume the obligation of making decisions.

"The following phrase is too often heard from the lips of educators:

" 'Children should not express their opinions.'

"To be sure, it is improper for a very young child to air his views on every subject, but it is also disastrous to forbid him to exercise his judgment.

"It is the duty of the tactful professor and

wise parents to teach the child a becoming reserve, a limited reserve, however, for it is indispensable that the pupil have the opportunity to practise forming an opinion on subjects within his comprehension.

"It is a great advantage to him when celebrated people discuss subjects with him, if only to aid him in forming his judgment, and to familiarize him with the thought of his relative importance.

"These discussions will have the further advantage of giving the child practise in expressing his thoughts clearly; for during these talks the master should watch him carefully to see that he does not express himself in common and inelegant language.

"When the child uses an inappropriate expression, the master should correct him, and aid him to find the one especially fitted to the idea he is attempting to express.

"Thus he will learn how to avoid being too wordy, and at the same time he will gain the habit of developing a subject without becoming fatigued.

"The master should be very particular to reprove stammering and hesitation of speech, for they generally lead to a vagueness of ideas.

"When a child finds a word difficult to pronounce, the master should make him repeat it slowly, and frequently.

"Children often pronounce certain syllables imperfectly. The best means should be employed, from the first, to teach them how to overcome these little faults.

"Let us acknowledge that these slight defects are often simply due to laziness on the part of the child, and the negligence of his parents, who are indifferent to them."

We must not lose sight of the fact that one of the most efficacious means of correcting this is eloquence.

Many cases of confirmed timidity originate solely in difficulty of utterance.

People who have not formed the habit of expressing themselves clearly, when young—those whose passing thoughts do not take a definite form—are paralyzed by the difficulty they experience in attempting to express themselves. They feel that they are inferior in arguing and in speech. Their thoughts, illy formed, are exprest prematurely, and their embarrassment increases in proportion as they feel the impossibility of expressing themselves.

This often causes hesitation, which generally

leads to the unfortunate habit of stammering.

If a person who feels himself in danger of forming this bad habit does not struggle hard to overcome the tendency, he will, without doubt, become timid, for the mortification that he would undergo would render him apprehensive of more trouble.

"It often happens that those unaccustomed from their infancy to choosing words which will express their thoughts properly, think of several expressions when they begin to speak, and, hesitating which one to use, commence a word, only to begin another, being undecided which one to employ.

"This results in people often expressing their thoughts so illy that they may be interpreted as offensive, or even contrary to the intended meaning.

"We can not insist too strongly," says Yoritomo, "on the importance of the following rule:

"Force the young to think clearly before they speak.

"Tenacious timidity often originates solely in a bashfulness that comes over one in the middle of a sentence, causing the rest of the sentence to be forgotten.

"Equivocal words do not express a definite

thought; they either escape one's mind, or so many inappropriate words come to mind at once, that the stammering speaker hesitates, not knowing which one to select, and, covered with confusion, his thought dwindles until it escapes him entirely.

"Oratorical debates between master and child are indispensable in cultivating skill in argument.

"At a later period, when students are brought before learned men to take examinations, those having had the advantage of such an education will readily take the lead, for, knowledge being equal, those who are able to state their views clearly, and express them eloquently, will be chosen as the favorite pupils."

In modernizing the thought of the savant one is forced to agree with him in thinking that success in an examination depends, not so much on the actual knowledge one candidate possesses, as on the fluent style of his thesis.

Many careers are closed to the timid, because of their inability to conquer their difficulty when confronted by examiners, who consequently thought that they knew nothing.

A well-recognized phenomena that afflicts the timid is spontaneous blushing, which, continually mounting to their cheeks in warm waves, marks them for the notice they so much fear.

This is very difficult to cure, because it is to apprehension itself that blushing is due.

A timid person rarely blushes when alone, unless recalling something that made him blush.

In which case the recollection of this episode infallibly results in this sign of confusion returning.

Nevertheless, the blush will not appear when the timid person feels that no one is looking at him.

The attack comes on solely because he says to himself, "I am going to blush," for he especially fears the deductions people might draw from this repeated blushing.

Once again Yoritomo, after having pointed out the evil, suggests a remedy.

"It is well," says he, "to check the propensity to blush suddenly, which afflicts some young people, as soon as it appears. These blushes, which are usually produced by nervousness, are generally caused because the timid person is conscious of having them, and that infallibly brings them on.

"I employed the means I am about to narrate to cure one of my young relatives of blushing.

"This method requires practise and perseverance on the part of educators, but it is infallible.

"Among my near relations is a young woman who is a model of virtue.

"However, all her good qualities were weakened by her great timidity, which caused her to blush on every occasion, tho she could give no reason for it.

"One day, when she was present, the conversation happened to be about a young *daimio* (noble), one of her friends, and her face turned purple, without any cause.

"Her mother, having unfortunately spoken to her about it, the young woman was most distrest, thinking that her name might be connected with that of the *daimio* on account of this causeless blush.

"From that day she lived in fear lest she would do it again. This fear led to the distressing idea that people might suspect her of having thoughts she never entertained.

"This led her to tremble and blush with fear whenever she imagined his name would be mentioned in the conversation.

"Her efforts to cure herself of this constant emotion were unavailing, owing to her timidity, and at last her health became impaired.

"She confided in me, and I undertook to cure her.

"I began, when we two were alone, to pronounce the name of the *daimio* unexpectedly, and her cheeks became purple. I let this crisis pass by, and after a quarter of an hour, I began again. I continued this until the attacks, which had gradually become less violent, ceased for that day.

"The next day I began again, after congratulating her on the success of the previous day.

"After several days this fear diminished, and she did not blush so often. When the blush appeared I pretended not to see it, and the young woman, convinced that it would no longer be noticed, gradually became cured of this particular emotion."

This is a method that seems very efficacious, and it should be successful, for timidity will always diminish if the occasions that produce it be skilfully repeated, until they cease to cause surprize, for the timid apprehend the unexpected.

"One should make it a point," says the venerable Nippon, "to cure the timid person of fear, which, if not conquered at once, will always increase. So much so, that to avoid the return of his bashfulness, he habitually avoids every occasion that will make him conspicuous.

"He becomes accustomed to taking an obscure place, not so much through modesty as through mistrust of himself, and the fear of being timid makes him so.

"At a very early age," says the philosopher, "children should also be taught to struggle with the problems of existence.

"How often in life will they be obliged to decide quickly, and well.

"They can not become accustomed too early to the consideration of the thousand and one little daily problems which they will evade, or magnify, according to the trend of their minds.

"It is always wise to let them take the initiative in such decisions. Stop arguing the question with them, if it presents difficulties beyond their comprehension.

"Another fault that very often makes people timid, is that of exacting that children shall be perfect.

"Besides, this makes them rebellious, or indifferent, and it almost always results in conscientious people becoming timid, for they despair of ever reaching the required goal, lose courage, and mistrust themselves.

"We must not labor under a delusion," says Yoritomo. "This is not due to pride; it is a sentiment that surely springs from a praiseworthy thought, but which nearly always interferes with the growth of the noble energy which should be the companion, and inspiration of earnest effort."

Another cause of timidity in children is the consciousness of a real, or an imaginary, affliction; for many parents erroneously think that they are rendering a service to their little ones in belittling, in their presence, the advantages that nature has bestowed on them.

In fact, if there is a real defect the educator should do all he can to make the afflicted persons consider it of not much consequence, if only for the purpose of keeping them from mistrusting themselves, a positive cause of inferiority.

If, on the contrary, the defect revealed consists solely in making them feel that they have no claims to good looks—whether this be true or not—simply for the purpose of preventing them from possibly becoming vain, still it, too, may have disastrous consequences.

Besides, beauty is a power. To pay no attention to it, or to deny it, is to deprive the child of a redoubtable weapon in the future combat of life.

Is it not more judicious to let him recognize this force, while at the same time suppressing vanity that might, at a later date, create unfortunate antipathies by inclining him to become presumptuous?

Timidity is too often confounded with reserve. A reserved person is conscious of his worth, and of his resources, which he concentrates, instead of scattering to the four winds.

Reserve is a force; timidity, a weakness; and success belongs to the strong.

LESSON III

TIMIDITY AND EXAGGERATED SELF-CONFIDENCE

"EXTREMES," as Yoritomo teaches us, "sometimes start from the same point; but, while in the first case the desired end is not attained, in the second, it is decidedly overreached.

"This is why one so often sees timid persons emerging from their mental seclusion, and—when under the influence of violent emotions such as anger, hatred, or love—going to extremes which a well-balanced man would never dream of.

"The reason of this anomaly is, that timidity being the lack of mental equilibrium, he who is obliged to make a special effort in order to express his sentiments by acts or gestures unfamiliar to him, loses sight of the consequences of his acts, because he is not accustomed to express his feelings."

This simple and profound definition explains the attitude of many timid persons, whose acts,

45

on certain occasions, are more daring than those
of men of well-balanced minds.

Furthermore, the timid usually nurse but one
thought, which they communicate to no one.
They do not perceive the gradual changes it
undergoes, and thus they become accustomed to
the new forms it assumes step by step, and adopt
it in its wildest transformation.

"If any one," says Yoritomo, "were to confine his thoughts forever to the bud just formed,
the bud would grow to be a large flower before
he would observe its growth, and transformation."

So it is with the timid person, who keeps his
thoughts to himself, and altho concentrating his
attention on them sufficiently to become ab-
sorbed by them, does not perceive that they are
gradually changing.

"But," one asks, "How is it that in 'Energy
in 12 Lessons' concentration is so greatly ex-
tolled, and here it seems to be censured?"

The answer is, that the concentration which
is the source of energy resembles only in name
the kind cultivated by the timid.

The energetic man concentrates his thoughts
so that he can rivet his attention on the objections, or the reasons which lead him to enter-

tain or reject a proposition; the timid man, on the contrary, permits ideas over which he exercises no control, and which are, in fact, often antagonistic to each other, to sink into his mind, and as his defect prevents him from asking any one's advice, he has no means of modifying his views.

Thus, by insidious degrees, which it is impossible for him to discover, he may entertain sentiments more pronounced than he is aware of.

"Solitude," continues the philosopher, "retards the flight of thought, which revolves round itself instead of soaring, untrameled."

This explains the tendency which timid persons have toward love of the marvelous. Being little more than observers of events in which their defect precludes their taking part, they comment on these occurrences to themselves, and unconsciously enlarge them, and shape them as they wish.

"When I was a child," he adds, "I was confined to my room for a long time with a severe illness. I was forbidden to read, and the only amusement I had was looking at the objects round me.

"The designs on a screen especially arrested

iII.3

my attention on account of the clusters of flowers, and the bundles of reeds.

"I passed hours studying them. Suddenly I
saw the outlines of eyes, but nothing more except a harmonious reproduction of nature.

"But, by degrees, the clusters of flowers became gardens, the reeds took on the imposing
aspect of a forest. In the gardens my imagination placed a princess, and in the forest, warriors.

"And now my tale began.

"Every new line I discovered became a pretext for me to create a personage. It was not
long before the princess was captured by a giant
—whom I saw—and the warriors advanced to
deliver her. Every day a panorama of per-
sonages passed before me, and varied the incidents in the story.

"The obsession became so strong that I spoke
of it in such a way that my parents were quite
anxious. The screen was removed, and a few
days later when they showed it to me again I
only saw what was painted on it.

"But the timid do not narrate the vagaries
of their inner vision and, no one being able to
guess the romance of the princess, they are not
set right, and so continue to see the princess

and the warriors where there are only sketches
of leaves and flowers.

"It often happens that this affection of the
will, which is the commencement of timidity,
seems like a great brilliancy; for the timid person is often ashamed of himself, and fears ridicule so much that—bad archer that he is—he
shoots his arrows beyond the target, through
fear of not reaching it."

This is a very usual case, and is especially
applicable to timid persons who feel that they
must play an important part.

The effort to make oneself conspicuous is
very great, for it must be constant, and consequently not natural to the timid, who are devoid
of will.

In order to satisfy this desire, the timid person, not having been able to force himself to
the front by assuming a steady attitude, is
obliged to greatly exaggerate the facts which he
wishes to make convincing.

Neither should we forget that as timidity
checks the will-power, no coherent and decided
action can proceed from it, but one is sure to see
actions of a somewhat explosive nature.

These explosions are often the result of a
torrent of thoughts and contradictory resolu-

tions, which the timid person has permitted to surge up within himself, but has not exprest.

"Water confined in a vase hermetically sealed," says Yoritomo, "may boil a long while without any one perceiving it, but at last it breaks the vase and spills over. Just so is it with the timid, who, having been represt, expand, through lack of self-control, and break forth in riotousness they are unable to control."

The vagaries which we listen to with a smile often spring from no other cause, and as it is impossible to prevent the vase from exploding and thereby permitting the water to escape, so it is useless for a timid person to attempt to suppress his foolish presumptuousness, which he exhibits on all occasions, just as tho he were tipsy.

And, in fact, it is a kind of intoxication. Emotion is a disorder that increases because the person subject to it feels that it is observed, and that it may be made the object of ridicule, and therefore he wishes to confound the chaffers, which facts cause emotion to pass through the two extremes of depression and exaltation, which give him, for the moment, the feeling of independence of will.

We must not forget that the timid person has

not full control over his muscles, and that the efforts he is obliged to make to bring them into subjection—unless he be accustomed to make these efforts—may lead to a disorder which often takes the form of exaggeration nearly approaching presumption.

As we shall see in the chapter which treats of timidity in regard to health, the timid person is almost always tortured by the desire to lie.

Sometimes these frequent lies are the direct result of a desire which haunts many timid persons, of viewing themselves from two different standpoints.

The person whose valiant deeds they recount is so far away, and so different from them, that they do not feel they are breaking through their own reserve in making use of this fictitious personage.

However, as the timid person is a weakling, the intoxication quickly spreads through his brain, and he indulges in flights of imagination which cause those who listen to him to doubt his word.

This usually makes him presumptuous. For the timid person is always sensitive.

No sooner does he see the smile of doubt on the lips of his listeners than he becomes very

angry, and tries to convince them he is telling
the truth, by piling up arguments pell-mell,
which he considers will prove his argument, and
exaggerating his statements in proportion as he
realizes the difficulty of forcing people to believe his statements.

Sometimes he, himself, feels the absurdity of
his assertions, but not having the intellectual
grasp necessary for beating an honorable re-
treat, instead of acknowledging himself vanquished he clings tenaciously to his improbable
views, and becomes so dissatisfied with himself
that he flies into a passion which increases to
the point of doing personal harm to those he
can not convince.

When the incoherent ideas permit the timid
person to remain conscient, his rambling remarks become extremely confused, but he considers it due to his self-respect to accentuate
them, instead of smilingly admitting that his
exaggerated statements had not illustrated his
point.

Another cause why the timid are presumptuous is, that in their hearts, they all desire to
remain unknown; most of them have two egos;
one that people scarcely know—for they are
very guarded in their confidences; and the

other which they find easier to show to the
world, for they know they are shamming, and
this knowledge gives them the same assurance
that a mask gives to those whose features are
hidden by it.

"I know," says Yoritomo, "a young man who
was exceedingly timid. One day he confided in
me, as follows:

"I feel within me a second ego, very different
from the first.

"One of them, the one which people know,
makes me suffer tortures on account of my
awkwardness, and the constant embarrassment
I experience from the uneasy state of mind and
the apprehension in which I live in consequence
of it.

"This ego I wish to expel, altho it is the only
one visible to the world.

"The other, 'ego,' 'my real self' is heroic.

"There is no act worthy of our bravest Sa-
mouraïs that it could not accomplish; it is generous, firm, brilliant; it commands admiration
from every one on every occasion.

"However, when this 'ego' which is so sincere
and so animated, tries to come to the front,
hidden forces oblige it to remain in the background.

"After making a prodigious effort I succeeded in expelling this ego, but I was distrest to see that these noble sentiments, great bravery, and high and generous impulses originated in absurd presumptuousness, which discovery plunged me in despair which it was impossible for me to curb, or guide."

I was obliged to hunt through the manuscripts a long while before finding the conclusion of this anecdote. And here is what I read on a page which I think must have been written some months later:

"It is with much interest that I am following the progress which Li-Hang-Tho is making toward gaining poise, and ultimate equilibrium. Under the influence of my advice his dual personality begins to disappear, and blend into a sort of intellectual unity, in which voluntary motions are gradually replacing automatic gestures.

"I prophesy the day will come when all paradoxical manifestations will cease, thanks to the supremacy of energy, and the power of concentrating the will, which, if carefully cultivated, will enable this young man to avoid the physical agony that afflicts the timid. For, being relieved from this constraint, he is, even

now, beginning to get control over his nerves
and to guard himself against fits of presumptuousness; faults to be deplored, as they all
place him in an equally false light.

It sometimes happens that people are presumptuous without knowing it. The timid person, owing to his defect, is not well informed
regarding the ordinary events of life, and as
soon as he attempts to describe them, he has the
same propensity as a child, of viewing them in
the light of the marvelous.

He also is like a child, in seeing an incident
in the most ordinary facts. His life, neces-
sarily very limited—mentally at least, because
he avoids every occasion of bringing himself to
the front—has not made him indifferent to the
thousand and one anxieties, or the little daily
happenings, for his character has kept him
aloof from these slight jars which end in a smile.
He makes everything a subject for thought, or
enthusiasm.

Should we be astonished that his nervous
system presents so many incongruities?

Certainly not. For his isolation prevents
him from cultivating politeness in his discussions.

If he were more accustomed to dealing with

ideas, he would have learned, like so many other
people, how to sustain and force his opinion in
accurate terms when face to face with those who
are opposed to him.

But, as he is accustomed to think alone, the
least divergence of opinion seems to him to be
a personal insult, and if he finds sufficient courage to take up this insult he does so by blustering, or by going to oratorical lengths which infallibly carry conviction to the minds of his
listeners.

The timid, as we have seen, readily become
presumptuous, and careless observers are apt
to attribute this to excessive boldness, when, on
the contrary, the afflicted person suffers solely
from the opposite defect, which is also a griev-
ous defect.

The usual result of this excessive presumption
is, that the timid person, when by himself, reviews with agony all the extravagant language
he has used; he revives every incident, hears
again all the replies, sees all the smiles, and,
by the sweat on his brow, he can tell how ridiculous he has appeared.

"Almost always," says Yoritomo, "after an
access of this sort, he relapses into a state of
uncontrollable apprehensiveness; for now he not

only fears other people, but himself, and the remembrance of his ridiculous adventure, which he recalls, and amplifies continually, increases his desire for solitude in which to hide his confusion.

At this point, it would be of incalculable value for him were he to come across some one who would sustain him, console him, and at the same time show him how to view things in their proper perspective, and who would also, in a way, lead him toward the equilibrium which renders life placid and harmonious.

Dramatic scenes, and great events are fortunately rare in the small occurrences which go to make up our existence.

Our lives consist, with few exceptions, in gray incidents which, from time to time, joy tints rose-color, and which grief temporarily dyes black.

Happy are those who can live a long series of years in the soft gray in which good intentions, reasonable ambition, the love of the duties belonging to their station in life have gathered round them, like a nimbus, the colors of hope and the aureole of success.

LESSON IV

TIMIDITY THE ENEMY OF HEALTH

TIMIDITY has many characteristic physiological results.

"It often has," says Yoritomo, "a very bad effect on the health, for the emotions to which the timid are subject are likely to endanger the bodily health.

"When developed sufficiently to cause the muscles to move at the caprices of the nerves, the result is a contraction, the repercussion often having disastrous effects.

"This contraction of the muscles makes the patient more timid, increases his bashfulness, and always results in his stammering, which, in very nervous people, and especially in neglected children, soon amounts to a serious defect.

"Let us take note that persons so afflicted press their lips together tightly, in proportion to the hold that their natural timidity has taken on them.

"Under the pressure of sentiments, among them the silent force we have just mentioned, the face and mouth muscles twitch in an uncontrollable manner.

"To these physical causes must be added the mental confusion which makes the patient all the more embarrassed when making unsuccessful attempts to enunciate distinctly.

"If the timid person does not take care he will soon be handicapped, and completely discomfited by this new phase of embarrassment, that overcomes him whenever he attempts to speak.

"The timid person, as we have already said, is, from the very nature of his defect, isolated; but he who is afflicted with stammering at last dreads all occasions that might cause him to display his infirmity.

"We also often see that stammerers become afflicted with hypochondria, which may be traced to the beginning of their timidity.

"There are many ways of curing stammering, and good results have been obtained from each, but the best way, the only infallible way, is by exercising a firm will, supported by energy.

"Now this is just what the timid lack, and that is why those who try to cure them must be more than patient and persevering, and determined.

"For no matter how efficacious be the treatment employed, it will not of itself succeed in curing the patient of his timidity which depresses him, and also makes it impossible for him to struggle successfully against himself.

"It is against himself that the timid must be especially protected, and this must be accomplished before attempting to restore him to health—in other words, to a mental state that will ensure bodily health. It is also necessary to forearm him against the frequent attacks of timidity that would interfere with the efforts made to cure him.

"Energetic action does more than any treatment to cure stammering.

"It is especially important to persuade the patient that he *can*, if he *will*, get rid of this serious inconvenience.

"Its cure depends more on the patient than on any assistance from without, we must admit, and this fact should be made clear to him.

"He should be made to feel thorough confidence in the person attempting to cure him.

"This is certainly one of the most delicate and difficult parts of the undertaking, for from the very nature of his defect, the patient is not apt to be communicative.

"He is usually inclined to lie, and on the rare occasions he holds forth he generally relates facts in such a way as to distort the truth.

"This, as we have remarked several times, originates in his desire to play a rôle. His disposition prevents him from acting as his imagination prompts, and thereby showing his worth; but he has done these things so often in his thoughts that it almost seems to him that he has actually done them.

"These partial lies are nearly always told regarding events he has witnessed, and in which his timidity has prevented him from taking the part he would have liked.

"From that fact, to thinking that he actually did what he had decided to do, and that he had spoken the words he dared not utter, there is only the difference between what we call a lie and what he calls stretching the truth.

"He narrates as a fact a thing he had fully determined to do. That is all.

"The timid person, as we have seen, owing to mental isolation, cultivates and matures extreme views, which remain unmodified because he is denied the advantage of discussing them.

"On the rare occasions when he is communicative, he is not slow to set up his opinions for standards, no one having convinced him of their worthlessness and their puerility.

"I had a friend," adds the philosopher, "who, tho a very able man, was misunderstood by nearly every one, because he was so timid that only his most intimate friends knew him sufficiently well to appreciate him.

"For after leaving a gathering in which he had failed to do himself credit, he always reviewed the phases of the argument, blaming himself for having lacked the courage to make the replies that came to his lips when alone, and also for not having spoken the repartee which he thought of now that his mind worked freely.

"Besides, he did not consider that he was telling a real lie when, in narrating what had taken place at the meeting the previous evening, he had stated as facts the learned opinions, the broad points of view, and the brilliant replies which he actally thought of, but had not exprest, owing to his timidity.

"One day, wishing to cure him of this defect which belittled him in my eyes, I tried to prove to him that at the meeting in which he pretended having played a brilliant part, he had in reality remained silent; and he replied as follows:

" 'It is true, that I said nothing, but having had all these thoughts, and most everything I said having been very personal, I feel justified in speaking as I do.' "

This very reasonable observation was summed up most appropriately in the last century in the following expression, "The spirit of the stairway."

For in fact it is only on the stairs, in other words, out of sight of the people whose presence paralyses him, that the timid person's mind works freely.

There it is that he reviews phases of the interview, being very much distrest to think he had appeared so dull as to merely dream what he intended to say; for being now relieved from restraint he forms opinions and thoughts, and readily finds words with which to clothe them.

If an appropriate phrase, a convincing argument, or a brilliant repartee occurs to him, he regrets still more that he did not speak out.

But as these words really embody his own thoughts he has no scruples in appropriating them, and even fondling them, and, on the rare
III.4

bccasions when he breaks through his extreme
reserve, he boasts, in good faith, that he exprest
these sentiments; never thinking that the people
who were present and knew that he had remained silent would feel like accusing him of
deception.

"A timid person," says Yoritomo, "is gifted
with fine perceptive faculties, but this profits
him nothing, because owing to his defect, he
does not generalize on what he observes.

"Many of the timid, however, who are unable
to make themselves felt in any other ways,
have left very remarkable manuscripts.

"But these are exceptional instances, for the
disposition accompanying timidity inclines the
patient, when far from public gaze, to magnify
his impressions, making it very difficult for him,
when writing, to separate facts from fancy. It
would be curious to examine from this point of
view the works which have come down to us
written by historians who have devoted their
lives to settling historical questions.

"The habit of amplifying and exaggerating
facts when narrating them generally originates
with the timid when they attempt to express
their own deductions and their own unaided
arguments."

Many timid persons are subject to cerebral affections; a great many also suffer from headaches which are specially likely to begin as soon as the patient awakens.

"These distressing symptoms can be traced to the contraction of the contributory nerves, making the patient more misanthropic, and annihilating the little will-power he would otherwise have had.

Excessive timidity produces troubles which are first cousins to insanity.

In proof of this we hear of timid persons who, when crossing over a space, were once so overcome by a feeling of loneliness, and of lack of protection, that they suffered excruciatingly, and dreaded placing themselves in a position likely to bring a return of these distressing symptoms.

At length it becomes a physical impossibility for them to overcome this fear, and whenever they cross an open space they stand still, tremble, and can not muster courage enough to conquer their fears.

If some one be with them the spell is at once broken, and they feel at ease when a relative or an old friend is by their side.

There are other timid persons who, when

writing, have writer's cramp as soon as any one looks at them.

Their fingers contract on holding the pen, and their wrists become rigid, in fact their entire arm becomes numb so that they can not write.

As soon as no one observes them these distressing symptoms disappear; they suffer no more pain, their wrists regain their suppleness, and they are able to write for some time without fatigue.

There are also a few timid persons who become paralysed with fright at the thought of eating before strangers.

Their mania originates in the exaggerated regard they have for the opinion of others, which slowly merges into a fear of being ridiculed. The mere fact of their thinking the gestures used in eating are not esthetic makes them wish to absent themselves from the table when others are present.

As time progresses this mania, like all the others, produces maladies known as phobies which are, alas! very closely related to madness.

"Another cause," says Yoritomo, "which is destructive to the health of the timid, is the palpitations that habitually accompany their attacks, sometimes resulting in seriously disturbing their physical well-being.

"As these troubles are usually accompanied by shortness of breath, and contraction of the muscles their repercussion on the heart may be disastrous."

And in addition to these well-vouched for statements, he makes a remark which does honor to his subtle knowledge of the human heart.

"May the Being who directs the universe," says he, "preserve the timid from illness, for their secretiveness holds them aloof from those who might be able to cure them.

"A timid person dares not speak of his ailment so as to give a doctor a clear idea of what the real trouble is.

"And he will even conceal it entirely if it be situated in certain parts of his body.

"Neither has he sufficient energy to follow the treatment necessary to effect a cure, or at least he is not persistent in carrying it out.

"If a timid person be forced to make a decision, he puts it off from day to day, until the evil has progressed so far that it is difficult to check.

"I knew a man who lived in a house situated on the edge of a large swamp. He devoted himself to metaphysical studies, and this, by separating him from the world, was the origin of a timidity that almost amounted to an illness.

"The effluvia that arose from that stagnant marsh in the late autumn had slowly undermined his health, and he had an attack of fever nearly every day.

"After some time I chanced to see him again, and I was so struck with the change that had come over him that I used all my influence to induce him to consult a physician.

"The physician's only command was, as I thought, for him to move away and live in a healthier locality.

"The duties of war having called me away about this time, I left him, after making him promise to obey the doctor's orders.

"I regretted to see that the thought of changing his residence was most distressing to his timid nature. In fact, he was somewhat frightened at the thought that he would have to make decisions, bestir himself and give orders.

"On my return, the following year, I had the misfortune to find him dying, and he confided to me what had prevented him from leaving the abode which was to become his tomb. He said it was because he was too 'bashful' to take the necessary steps to install himself anew.

He had not dared to look for another place, being paralysed with fear at the thought of the necessary discussions that would arise; and he had been so greatly disturbed at the thought of arranging to have his manuscripts removed that he put it off from day to day hoping that on the following day he would feel sufficient energy to undertake all these things which seemed to him so overwhelming.

"A short time after this he died, a victim of the timidity which had made him lead a miserable existence, and at last caused his death.

"This defect, as it regards health, amounts to a real crime when it affects, in a more or less degree, the health of other people.

"We see children suffering in consequence of their parents hesitating to tell the doctors of certain disorders, because they are in parts of the body which they feel 'ashamed' to mention.

"Other little ones have contracted serious illnesses because their parents have taught them to be 'ashamed' to ask for the advice necessary in attending to nature's needs.

"No one can tell how many timid persons there are, for they are usually overlooked.

"The doctors merely state officially that such a person died of such a malady, but they rarely trace the illness to its origin; and yet there is an axiom in therapeutics which no doctor should forget, which is, 'That before attempting to cure the evil, the cause must be ascertained and removed; and this is the only successful method of procedure.'"

To illustrate this the philosopher tells us one of his anecdotes, which give zest to his precepts.

"There was a man," he says, "who owned some rice-fields which he inherited from his father.

"One day he noticed that the darnel had made its appearance on his land, and he made it his business to cut the weeds down.

"But the field was quite large and it took him a great many days; in fact so long that when he thought his task finished he noticed that the weeds had begun to grow again in the part of the field in which they had been first cut down.

"So he began over again, but this time instead of pulling up the darnel by the roots, thereby running the risk of uprooting some of the rice plants, he cut it down, and so it multiplied more rapidly than before.

"It soon spread so fast that the good grain

was smothered, and there was scarcely more than a few feet of green to be seen.

"It was a very scanty crop, and the following year the noxious weeds—their roots not having been dug out and burned—had multiplied to such an extent and were so thrifty that there was not space enough for a single grain of rice.

"Many people resemble the man in this anecdote; they realize the danger and take active measures to prevent it, but having neglected to ascertain the causes, or even if they know them, taking no means to suppress them, tho their efforts seem to be intelligently directed, the evil continues to grow to such proportions that it is impossible to extirpate it, for it has permeated the entire system just as the darnel covered the entire fields.

"Regarding timidity, it is indispensable to ascertain its causes.

"Most physical ailments have mental origin.

"Therefore no stone should be left unturned to combat not the malady itself—which, unless it be very acute, will cure itself as soon as the causes that produced it be removed—but the sources of the illness which, by taking patient and energetic measures will also soon be removed.

"Timidity, as every one knows, precludes physical exertion, and it is an undeniable fact that a determination to get well is the principal requisite in regaining one's health.

"To uproot evil is good, but to prevent it is better; and since timidity causes so many physical inconveniences, it must be overcome, in order to realize that first requisite for happiness—a sane mind in a healthy body."

LESSON V

TIMIDITY AND FAMILY LIFE

"It is a remarkable fact," says Yoritomo-Tashi, "that it is the *daimios* (nobles) whose timidity prevents them from distinguishing themselves in the *genroïn*, (senate) or in the *sanjun* (state council) who are most feared by their families.

"It would seem as tho, when with people who put them at their ease, they give vent to their anger, caused by realizing to what a disadvantage they appear when in public.

"They are especially fond of making excuses for themselves and in venting on others the ill humor caused by the vexations inherent in their defect.

"If humiliated in public they return home in a rage and make every one miserable.

"Their dissatisfaction with themselves makes them so irritable that no one can stand them, and they usually let it out in the bosom of their families.

"For as the timid person is always lacking

in will-power, it is impossible for him to control himself sufficiently to avoid these outbursts, which he usually deplores.

"I said 'usually,' tho he often does not care.

"Some timid persons, when at home, are purposely violent, for their minds being dwarfed by lack of volition, they mistake these demonstrations for courage.

"When with those belonging to them, and with whom they consequently feel at their ease, they try to indemnify themselves for the passive and inferior position they are obliged to assume before strangers.

"The effrontery, ridicule, and veiled sarcasm of the latter, act as so many stimulants inducing the timid to regain a good opinion of themselves, and to boast that they possess the qualities they consider the most desirable, in other words, firmness and decision.

"But we can not repeat too often that the timid—being especially devoid of will-power—has no mental poise, and therefore he readily transforms the qualities he only perceives in a one-sided way, into intolerable vices."

Many centuries after Yoritomo lived, Nietzsche spoke of reticence, an affliction peculiar to the timid.

It is in the family life that this sentiment is exhibited in its most trying form.

The timid person is not in touch with the members of his family, no matter how much he loves them.

The fear of being awkward makes him dread being demonstrative, and often when his heart is melting with tenderness, he would feel so embarrassed were it to be seen, that he avoids showing any marks of affection in his family. Too often, by making a brusque gesture, he stops short an exhibition of affection which he has not the courage to return as his heart prompts.

Should we feel suprized if the members of his family, chilled by what they consider indifference, gradually imitate him and become less demonstrative, as they find their advances awaken no echo in his heart?

And so the timid person entrenches himself every day within the fortress of his infirmity, and grows more lonely and more misunderstood.

His lack of the sentiment of protecting others —such a strong family tie—not only affects him, but his family also.

Children, who are quick to perceive the outward signs of courage and decision, gradually lose the respect they should have for the head of the family; for they do not consider this awkward, embarrassed and hesitating man qualified to conduct them through life. They imagine that he would be vanquished by the first obstruction, and drag them down with him.

Young persons, whose reasoning powers are not fully developed, do not state this fact clearly as I have done; nevertheless, children do not look up to the timid head of a family, and by degrees they divest him of all right to command.

How can he regain the control he should exercise over his children when the question comes up of choosing their vocation, or how can he preserve them from the pitfalls of adolescence?

The most usual result, and one to be deeply deplored, is that it makes children—their impulsiveness being represt by coldness—confide in strangers.

It frequently happens that through lack of experience they fall into the hands of unreliable advisors whose counsels are often pernicious.

But even when their friends are well chosen the family unity is none the less broken, for unity of thought, which prospers on the mutual interests, mutual remembrances, similar responsibilities, reciprocal affection, which constitute the basis of family life, are always obliterated when an outside influence, no matter how good it may be, strikes a strange note in the symphony of family life.

"On the side of a hill that protects the city from the north winds, there was," says Yoritomo, "a spot where I loved to rest after the fatigue of giving orders.

"There the convolvulus wound itself so tightly round the branches of the old trees that scarcely a leaf could force its way through the exuberant foliage of this vegetable parasite.

"These trees, whose roots jutted out from the hill here and there, were my especial favorites. Their branches, like long arms, made good supports for the overhanging convolvulus which they seemed to display for our admiration, like a superb and sparkling drapery. On warm days the birds would nestle there and chirp. Even the weakest of these trees held itself erect under its royal garb.

"Some of them were nearly dead, not a drop of sap was left in them, and yet they held themselves erect, thanks to the powerful bracing given them by the supple filiaments which had at first clung to them for protection, and now, in their turn, gave them substantial support.

"There were also other trees, more delicate, somewhat bent by the weight of the vine which nearly touched the ground, and threw out tendrils toward the next tree of a stouter build, thus forming a dome of verdure which, on the following summer, I was pleased to see had grown thicker and more mysterious.

"But one day just after a storm I was sorry to see that the moving dias of silk had been destroyed.

"The weakest trunks had been split, and later broken off, and the delicate convolvulus which they had dragged down with them, encircled the feet of the traveler, and was so muddy, and torn by insects as it lay on the ground that it looked like a mass of rags.

"Other trees, that, owing to their strength, or the interlocking of their supple branches, had been able to withstand the storm, still gave their gentle support to the graceful burden whose fragile but exuberant growth had been its safeguard.

"This seemed to me to be very symbolic of the family.

"While family rule is firm and decided, children lean on the persons representing it, and if need be entwine themselves so closely round him as to hide his age and his decrepitude.

"However, if the support be too weak to weather the storms of life, his defeat drags down those by whom he is surrounded.

"The timid resemble those trees which can neither give the necessary support to the frail convolvulus, nor derive the necessary support from it; having been overcome by the storms of life they drag down with them the vines they were unable to protect.

"It also often happens that children feeling that they are not protected as they should be, turn away from the head of the family, when he is vacillating and of weak will-power, and lean on others whose poise inspires them with a confidence which their natural protector has not been able to exert.

"Nevertheless, no matter how salutary the influence of the outsider may be, it must always be regretted that it is not encouraged by him who should, in connection with the teacher, mold the soft wax of the youthful minds, his own offspring, so that in addition to acquired virtues they would be led to cultivate the virtues inherent in the family, which are best furthered by recalling the great deeds of one's ancestors. III.5

"Or even if one's ancestors have not played a prominent part in history they should be honored for their unselfishness, devotion, and the kindness they displayed within the family circle.

"These noble deeds are all the more meritorious because they are only seen and appreciated by those near by, and they are all the more difficult to accomplish, for they do not call for brilliant effort, fostered and rewarded by pride and glory, but rather for constant endeavor under the shadow of obscurity, and a devotion the result of which is only appreciated by the few persons who witness it.

"These efforts, admired because they originate in the will and are accomplished by energy, are such as the life nobly lived exacts from every one who aspires to the distinction of being called a good man.

"But, as I have already said, strangers have no means of knowing these facts, and if the head of the family does not instruct the children regarding them, even the essence of the family virtues will evaporate, and before long a disintegration will begin, slight at first, but nevertheless sufficient to modify the qualities that constitute the characteristic strength of this family."

After these commentaries, so clearly set forth,
it seems as tho one could add but little to the
arguments of the ancient philosopher, Nippon;
but let us hear what he has to say regarding
marriage, and the choosing of a vocation; two
acts upon which the happiness of the family
usually hinges.

"The timid person," says Shogun, "is rarely
happy in his married life, he nearly always
marries a woman chosen for him, instead of one
of his own choice.

"He finds it so difficult to express his sentiments that he hesitates, stammers, and is as
awkward as possible, for he realizes what an
absurd impression he is making, and he is
greatly pained when he sees, or thinks he sees,
in the eyes of the young girl, or her parents to
whom he is speaking, a derisive smile which
completely disconcerts him.

"A timid person rarely marries except
through the intermediary of an obliging or an
interested friend. Therefore, it often happens
that he views the woman he has not chosen, and
who can never understand him, with indifference if not with antipathy.

"Quite often serious quarrels originate in a
misunderstanding which might have been easily

explained away in the beginning. But a timid person has no knack of saying conciliatory words; so he takes refuge in silence, which nearly always makes him brusque or sulky, and so the quarrel grows day by day.

"I had," says Yoritomo, "a friend whose timidity drove him to despair. After making some attempts to cure himself, which were retarded by the very nature of his defect, he confided in me occasionally when he had courage enough to open his heart.

"In this way I learned how deeply he loved a daughter of the Samurai Thang-Hong. He had been captivated by her soft voice and her graceful bearing, which made the crudeness of her sister all the more conspicuous, for she resembled an amazon more than a charming young lady.

"He even felt rather an aversion toward this sister, therefore he thought he would not like to be obliged to live in the family of the girl he had decided to marry.

"What was my surprize, on returning from a journey, to find him married to this very woman whom he pretended to detest.

"So I hunted him up, and when we were alone I asked him to tell me what had caused this sudden change of feeling.

"Alas! no change had taken place; he still loved, in sorrow and in secret, the woman of his choice, but never having had the courage to say so, the other sister, who was desperately in love with him, made such overtures to him that he had not the heart to undeceive her regarding his own sentiments.

"And so he led a joyless existence, between one woman he detested, and another, who quite unconsciously made him suffer greatly, for she had married, and so my friend experienced all the tortures of jealousy."

Love is almost always very nearly allied to suffering as far as the timid person is concerned, for he is beguiled by dreams—as he dare not express his views—which often plunges him in the deepest despair, caused by regrets.

Because the timid head of the family has suffered and is suffering daily from his defect it is especially necessary for him to do everything in his power to prevent any one belonging to him from being so afflicted.

Should he not feel equal to undertaking this cure himself, he ought to place the education of his children in the hands of a teacher able to develop in these young minds the qualities which are indispensable in the struggle of life;

a struggle which begins with our first lessons
and only ends with life.

The moral support of an enlightened master
is especially necessary for the children of the
timid father, who generally gives them but indifferent advice, and whose judgment is rarely
impartial.

His mental isolation, by causing him to live
a life within himself, and which no one else
knows anything about, often makes his ideas
impractical; but he will not admit that they
are not sound, he thinks them reasonable, and
he is quite ready to criticise severely any one
who differs from him.

There are also many circumstances in which
the child, grown to maturity, and feeling the
necessity of seeking protection from outsiders,
clings to his teachers, and tries to make them
take an interest in him, and seeks a calling
that will give him the opportunity of practising
the knowledge he has gained, or of exercising
his special proclivities, or he obtains introduc-
tions to persons whose influence may facilitate
his entrance into a certain career.

"This is the moment," says the philosopher,
"when the head of the family should display
devotion, solicitude, and tact, gifts that should

be possest by every one having charge of guiding the mind."

And he adds:

"Only a father can show his son the imperceptible line of demarcation that divides the aplomb of the upper classes of society from boldness, a very common fault in people who do not amount to much."

Timidity in the master of the house is especially unfortunate in family life, when the time comes to give the children the orientation which will guide them in choosing a career.

It is almost impossible to discern the real bias of young persons for they are very enthusiastic, and impulsive, and impressionable to both good and bad influences.

Long talks induce young people to be communicative, which makes them more willing to listen to advice, these talks also gradually invite confidence, and in fact they furnish every clue in ascertaining what vocation they should choose, for the knowledge that a parent should have regarding his children is a closed book to the timid, who have no gift for gaining the confidence of the young.

Should we be astonished if, under these circumstances, the young man, given over to his

false theories, tries to put them into practise
by plunging into a career which will not permit
of his developing his special proclivities?

In every condition of life timidity is a blem-
ish, but in family life it becomes a grave fault,
where it constantly and passively restrains
energy, the source of moral harmony, the highest
goal that can be reached.

LESSON VI

TIMIDITY THE PARENT OF ENVY

PEOPLE very rarely examine themselves critically enough to see their faults.

Even if they do see them, it is still more unusual for them to seek to cure them, or even to diminish them.

On the other hand many people are very indulgent to faults which they can not disclaim.

Let us remark that people simply excuse their faults by bringing up all sorts of extenuating circumstances which are only so many pretexts for deferring their efforts toward improving them.

So that, instead of subjecting themselves to a rigid examination, and struggling bravely to correct their faults, they are weak enough to evade them.

We often, through inertia, persuade ourselves that the fault in question is not so bad as we imagined.

Becoming accustomed to it, we soon view it

as just one of those little faults which people smile at and say, "Man is not perfect!"

As it is wearisome to struggle, and difficult to climb the hill, and as our attempts to affect a cure make but slow progress when aimed amiss by a vacillating will, we sink again into a comfortable indifference, closely related to cowardice.

But as the venerable Shogun says, this peace is not enjoyed by the timid. We are often too well-satisfied with ourselves, but the timid rarely experience this feeling.

"If they do not struggle against their dejection they will be severely punished for their negligence.

"That is why we rarely find the timid friendly.

"They are more or less a prey to the envy which enters their hearts when they realize their obscurity, and contrast it with the success of others.

"Some people find it very trying to witness the success of others.

"However, even people whose minds do not soar to the highest plain often feel no bitterness in regard to the success of others, for they do not think it will interfere with their own.

"Let us add that they always believe that their success will be owing to their own superiority.

"There are then but few reasons why envy should be permitted to accomplish its hateful work in the heart of the timid, for they feel confident that their own success is at hand.

"Most of them see, not only their own efforts crowned with success, but the weakening, if not the effacement of their neighbors' prerogatives.

"The timid can readily give their support to others and can admire them also, for they consider this as but merely being patronizingly polite, in other words a coin that people filled with self-conceit willingly distribute to those they regard as competitors of but little account.

"This egotistical generosity is unknown to persons tainted with timidity.

"They are consumed with mortification at not being able to shine in their turn, and if they have ability they are furious at the thought of being powerless to display it.

"From having an exaggerated idea of their own importance, to execrating those whose self-possession brings them to the front, is but a step, and this step quickly taken brings them to the cavern in which envy grovels.

"If the timid were only to reason a little they would see that the comparison they draw is not worth much, for they would only have to exert their will to display the very qualities they attribute to themselves.

"Serious introspection would show them their faults, spur them on to overcome this obstacle, to take their proper place, and lead them to equal, if not to excel, those they view with such contempt.

"They are perfectly aware of the necessity of struggling against this infirmity which, no matter what their worth or their attainments may be, relegates them to remain forever in the background.

"Envy is not a monopoly of the timid, but in them it flourishes, because they mingle so little with others that their minds do not expand.

"Then, too, as it is impossible for them to express their ideas, they can not modify them by getting advice, and so their unjustifiable aversion remains unchecked.

"Their mental solitude soon results in their becoming eccentric, so that the slightest gesture of the person they hate, the least thing they do, adds to the flame, and makes the patient suffer as tho they had intentionally annoyed him.

"But instead of complaining, and telling some one about his suffering, which could certainly be cured by good advice, they shut it up in their hearts, in which hatred is sown and flourishes as a seed of grain fallen on land protected from the gale.

"A timid person, when envious, merely hates and suffers.

"Tho he dreads the thought of grieving alone he is fully aware of the meanness of this feeling; being too undemonstrative to seek the ameliorations which would expand his mind he avenges his grievances on every one round him provided he is not embarrassed.

"For impulsive persons most naturally treat others to their ill-temper, brought on by dissatisfaction with themselves.

"In the unmerited reproaches which they fling at their families they feel as tho they were extenuating their faults which, being too weak to correct, they display daily.

"But these unmerited rebukes, always in the end lessen the ties of sympathy, already so light, which bind the timid to their families, and so there often springs up a feeling of mutual constraint which originated in their not understanding or appreciating one another.

"And, as no one round them knows what sentiments bring on these strange attacks of temper, their friends find it impossible to avoid making allusions, or expressing thoughts that make their wounds bleed afresh.

"Timidity in a child is not nearly so serious, for by great care and a little tact parents can nearly always conquer it.

"They should know how to gain his confidence, and by showing their affection repress his evil tendencies, and encircle him with their protection.

"This done, they can very readily destroy the bad leaven of envy within him; for an evil unconcealed is easily cured.

"Many children are mortified because they feel their weakness in the presence of strength; this wounds their self-esteem, and readily engenders envy.

"In a case like this it is the duty of the teacher to inspire the child with self-confidence by praising the qualities he possesses, and which the person he is jealous of lacks.

"In a word, the first step must be to destroy the feeling of inferiority which causes the timid to become envious.

"This, however, is a very difficult task, for

care must be taken not to go to the other extreme by letting him have too high an opinion of himself.

"One can not imagine how very ingenious the timid are in inventing excuses for their faults.

"Few of them are willing to acknowledge that they are envious. Let us add that they are usually sincere in denying this fault.

"However, if their violent temper does not drive away those who could give them advice, they should recognize the fact that the persons they have an antipathy for are especially those who display the qualities which their timidity denies to them.

"A man who is brilliant, a good conversationalist, and of a fine figure will always be disliked by the timid.

"They also hate those who have done brave deeds in war," adds Yoritomo, "and this hatred is accentuated in proportion as they become weaker and more cowardly."

The following pages bring a smile to the lips of the reader when he considers that, notwithstanding the great differences of climate, costumes, and nationalities, the psychology of the feminine heart has scarcely changed for centuries.

For, in the manuscript entitled "Envy, and Timid Women," we find the subject treated in a manner which would hold its own in one of our most up-to-date Parisian reviews.

"Women," says he, "are much more liable to become envious through spite, for timid women always hate other women who are conspicuous for their beauty and their elegant clothes.

"Besides, they think they have found a very easy way of belittling the physical attractions of those whose prominence offends them, when they naïvely imagine that by not recognizing these attractions they annihilate them.

"When they have decreed that such and such friends can lay no claim to beauty, they not only almost think they have destroyed that beauty, but most of them think that by this procedure they enhance their own merit, which thrives on borrowed glory."

The observations of Shogun remain true after all these years.

But in our time we have another kind of envy to consider besides that incited by external advantages, and that is jealousy of intellectual superiority.

This sentiment explains the ostracism which

women have long exercised toward those of their number who devote themselves to any form of art.

The enlightened views of the latter give offense to the dulness in which the timid, and women who lack will-power, are immersed forever.

They do not realize the daily drudgery and anxiety necessary in struggling to attain and to keep a footing in the foremost ranks. Timidity, the dread of exerting themselves, or their ignorance, prevent them from trying to emulate others. They prefer rather to run down the reputation of others than to enter the arena in their turn and fight with them, side by side.

But, nevertheless, this somewhat platonic reasoning does not satisfy the timid, for, in denying most emphatically that any one else is superior to themselves, they do so somewhat as the fox in the fable, who pronounced the grapes too green.

Like the fox, they can not help throwing an envious glance toward the good things they can never possess, and their ill-humor thrives on the great vexation they feel at not being able to equal those they affect to deprecate.

Most timid persons could easily appear as
III.6

brilliant and become just as renowned as the people who excite their jealousy; but to accomplish this they would have to emerge from their solitude and mix with the crowd.

The timid can not bear the thought of exerting themselves sufficiently to compete with others. They prefer to cede the place to those whom they could readily have outstript had they been sufficiently energetic, and so they conceive a spite which soon degenerates into envy.

It is absurd to pretend that the detestable fault called envy can promote emulation, the friend of progress.

This subtle justification of a belittling sentiment can only serve as an excuse to those who are envious through timidity.

Emulation is the desire to attain to the highest, leading one to take the steps necessary to outstrip one's rivals.

"The indispensable conditions for those who wish to outstrip their competitors in merit and bravery is," as we are told, "to cherish no illusions regarding themselves.

"If too complaisant, they soon become overconfident, and feel that they have a better chance than others of gaining the desired virtues.

"But if they acknowledge that they have not yet reached perfection, their judgment regarding others will be so one-sided that they really think that their competitors are their inferiors, and that they can outstrip them without making any effort.

"In the rare instances in which they are honest with themselves and acknowledge that they would have to make a great effort to reach the same point attained by those of whom they are jealous, their timidity, reticence, and the embarrassment which they are sure to feel prevent them from taking a high standing.

"To outstrip others we must emerge from our apathy and attract attention to ourselves, and a timid man can not bear the thought of facing his equals.

"The mere feeling that a stranger is near paralyses him, and the thought of acting, speaking, appearing in public, taking examinations, stating his views before his teacher, or giving an address on matters of State before an assembly causes him to suffer so terribly that he can not bear to think of it.

"The timid person is, therefore, excluded from all competitions, whether he be merely a young student or a man who should command respect for his bravery in war and the weight of his arguments in furthering the good of the State.

"There are many other reasons why he will have to stand apart from militant life; the most conspicuous of these is—for we are now discussing the timid person who is envious as well— the propensity for hating without cause.

"The timid person always hates instinctively. This hatred in the beginning is a mere impression; he sees, or thinks he sees, a smile, and he imagines that the smile is caused by making fun of him on account of his awkwardness; or else he notices that silence reigns as soon as he made his appearance, so he comes to the conclusion that he is being slandered.

"This seed of hatred once sown in his heart is not slow to bear its fatal fruit. Shortly, every word, every action of the persons he hates, their good nature, their seriousness, and, indeed, every attitude they strike seems to him a personal insult.

"If they be gay, he thinks they are making merry at his expense; if sad, he attributes it to awkwardness; and if they are effusive he thinks they are too loquacious, and so he resents it.

"What began as a mere impression, the lonely mind of the timid person transforms into a sus-

picion which soon turns into hostility, and, secretly aided by his imagination, he transforms
hostility into hatred, all the more tenacious because he is afraid to let it be seen.

"A timid person's reasons for hating are
many and indefinite.

"Sometimes even the mere fact of his having
felt ill at ease in the presence of a stranger
makes it impossible for him to see the man
again without an antagonistic feeling.

"If the stranger happens to have witnessed
one of the piteous exhibitions peculiar to the
timid, the timid man magnifies it until he suffers agony from his embarrassment, and unconsciously lays the blame on the stranger.

"The timid person is an easy prey for
schemers, who take advantage of his dread of
coming to the front by sparing him the thousand and one little steps that frighten him.

"He did not choose his friends. He lets
them impose on him, and he often becomes very
fond of people who constantly deceive him.

"Sometimes he has true friends; but on account of his stubborn and reticent character it
is difficult for him to keep his friends, and,
therefore, he is mostly surrounded by those
who are guided by interested motives.

"In this case, the friend who is trying to further his own interests does not try to affect a cure; on the contrary, he contrives to keep his victim in this state because by so doing he favors his schemes. He speaks in his stead, spares him from having to take the steps he dreads, acts for him, decides for him, and even saves him the trouble of thinking for himself.

"To sum up, he comes to the front on every occasion that makes life insupportable for the timid person, and thereby aids him in sinking into a nonentity.

"These friendships encourage envy in the timid person, for his wily friend fans the flame that serves his purpose so well, by estranging him from all his friends.

"That is how he lights the flame of hatred in the heart of him he is exploiting, and he takes good care that the timid man be kept away from all those who might have a noble, tender affection for him.

"Is envy in timid persons incurable?

"Certainly not, but it is a very difficult task, for to endear oneself to them we must be able to read their thoughts and to perceive their generous sentiments which they hide from the casual observer.

"Nevertheless, it is a noble mission to bring
them to a higher plain of thought, for hatred
is a terrible burden to carry, and it must be
very gratifying to see it vanish by degrees,
giving place to kind-heartedness with which the
energetic are so familiar, and which they cultivate because it creates an inward joy, and makes
life serene."

LESSON VII

ESTHETICISM AND TIMIDITY

Tho this word has but recently come into use, what it stands for is eternal.

"This instinct, contrary to all others," says Yoritomo, "does not originate in conversations, nor in the vague impetus of self-defense that determines most of our actions or our impulses.

"It originates in a state of mind in which one is satisfied to look at what seems to bring him nearer to perfection.

"It is a flight toward the ideal; it is in a way collaborating with the Creator, since our spirit has the power to evolve something charming by means of the necessary implements, etc.

"A painter who takes a paint-brush and a piece of canvas and paints a picture which calls forth enthusiastic admiration; a musician who accompanies on his flute the story of the noble deeds of warriors—provided they are able to thrill our hearts with the same enthusiasm

that animated those whose prowess they recall,
are the creators, while we are the collaborators.

"One need not take an active part in order to
play this last rôle; it suffices to feel within oneself the emotion which for a moment unites our
soul to its Maker.

"This emotion is the real social leveling; for,
granting that the main aim in life is to embellish
it as much as possible, it has been ascertained
that the most dejected when admiring a landscape, or looking at a sunset; listening to the
harmonies of music, or watching rhythmic
dances, feel an intoxication of joy the memory
of which will brighten the hard days of labor."

Every one, no matter in what condition of life
he be, should strive after the beautiful.

"The great teachers from the earliest an-
tiquity devoted their attention especially to
this, and the masterpieces they have left us
more than prove what importance the ancients
attached to the beauty of posture.

"This special beauty has the advantage over
others in that it can be acquired by every one.

"We are not born with it. It is rather the
result of habits formed in early childhood by
teachers who cultivate the beautiful.

"For harmony of posture, which is one of

the most perfect forms of beauty, is not possible in the timid.

"Their movements are always circumscribed, and timorous. They never gain the ease they admire so much in those who are not afflicted with this fault.

"Can harmony of gesture be acquired? Can an artistic attitude be cultivated, as a fine voice?

"Yes, provided one be careful to guard children, from their most tender age, from everything that might curb their natural grace, and watch to see that they do not use common gestures.

"But they should be especially guarded against timidity.

"What charm can we see in those who are frightened at nothing and who do not possess sufficient self-control to take pains to be graceful in their movements, and who, in fact can scarcely regulate them?

"What beauty can we expect to see in a person who is afflicted with a disorder he is incapable of surmounting?

"Do people when drowning think about striking beautiful attitudes when they are struggling for their lives?

"Children must, therefore, be guarded

against becoming timid if they are to take part in this manifestation of beauty which finds expression in harmony and rhythm.

"Why should they distress people by their affected and ungraceful movements?

"It is criminal to allow this fault to develop in the young, for it will deprive them of a great deal of pleasure.

"Of what use is it for them to be gifted by nature, if their timidity—which is nearly always an acquired fault—prevent them from appearing at their best and so pleasing every one?

Before inspiring the child with a desire for striking familiar attitudes gracefully it is well to show him how he can attain to the self-control required to develop sufficient will-power and energy.

"That done, he should be imbued with the importance of harmony, not only in movements of the body, but in the workings of the inner life.

"Sometimes the least thing will sow the seeds of timidity in the mind of the young.

"In this category we must place the wrong parents do their children when, for the sake of economy, they make them wear old-fashioned garments that cause them to look ridiculous.

"The parents can not be blamed for not in-
culcating in them a taste for very elegant things,
but neither should they, under pretense of
saving, make their children wear clothes too
out of date, or too conspicuous.

"Youth is relentless, exercising no forbear-
ance; and the child when ridiculed by his play-
mates can not help but notice it, and he consequently suffers keenly."

Does it not seem as if these words were
spoken by a contemporary!

If this be true in a country and an age when
costumes changed but little, how much more
true it is now!

The beginning of a persistent timidity can
often be traced to the confusion a child feels
when he says, "I'm not like other children."

The jeers in which his comrades indulge on
seeing him in a costume evidently made by in-
experienced hands have often annoyed him so
much that he soon became bashful.

If this pupil be obliged to step forward to
take examinations or to speak, the feeling that
people are looking at him and making fun of
him increases his awkwardness.

And as timidity is increased through the fear
the patient has of showing it, the details which

make one smile may have an enormous influence lasting throughout life.

We can not conceal the fact that it is more difficult to strike a graceful attitude in an absurd costume than in one's ordinary clothes.

It is the parents' duty to see that their children's clothing be neat, if not costly. In this way they can spare the children not only little passing annoyances, but the evil tendencies resulting from wounded self-esteem.

There is also another reason, more difficult to define, but none the less real, which should cause parents to reflect when dressing their children in old-fashioned finery.

This reason is illustrated by the venerable Shogun in a very graphic manner.

"Warriors have a motive," says he, "for covering their faces with hideous masks. Tho their principal thought is to strike terror into the hearts of the enemy, they also try to pattern their souls after their warlike trappings.

"Has any one ever seen a man going to battle taking a lamb as his emblem?

"We always assume some of the characteristics of the person whose costume we wear, and the child drest in ridiculous garments unconsciously strikes uncouth attitudes, besides, taunted at the fun leveled at him, he frequently takes refuge in embarrassment, which results in his hating those who have caused him to suffer and also his parents who were the indirect cause of it.

"In every age dress has been an important question.

"Some costumes betoken authority; their shape is imposing, they necessitate dignified gestures which induce gravity of manner, and which reflect on the minds of those who wear them.

"Other costumes, like military uniforms, suggest violent action and incite those who wear them to acts requiring quick decision and dashing resolutions."

These remarks are especially applicable to our own country where the greatest variety of costumes can be seen daily, thereby illustrating more fully what I have said.

A peasant when drest in his Sunday best is less rough and more refined than usual.

The fear of spoiling his clothes counts for something, but we must acknowledge that it has an influence over him and tones him down, at least temporarily.

There is a Japanese proverb which says: "A

beautiful soul is rarely reflected in an ugly face."

This proverb does not, of course, refer to classic beauty, but if we define beauty as serenity and harmony, the proverb holds good.

A beautiful soul always expresses itself by some outward sign; for instance, a mild expression, a sweet smile, freedom of gesture, sincerity of speech, etc.

We read further on that "symmetrical attitudes should be supplemented by a musical voice, and conversation to correspond.

"The good looks of the most beautiful woman in the world are soon forgotten unless she can charm by her conversation.

"The fascination of a beautiful face diminishes when we see it often, but that of a charming conversationalist lasts forever, for it is constantly being renewed.

"That is the reason we should be more particular to see that children have some self-assurance which with appropriate gesticulations is the foundation of the art of speaking.

"But if we wish to succeed we must not fall into the error of most educators.

"Under pretext of accustoming children to speak in public they begin by teaching them to

learn verbatum, to recite stories in language they
do not understand, and to accent them with gestures so awkward that they make one smile.

"'How absurd!' we say, on witnessing the
awkward mimicry of the child.

"The fact is too often overlooked that if this
'absurdity' be not remedied at once the child
will become so accustomed to these studied attitudes that when he is grown and speaking
before an audience he will still accent his remarks by making the studied gestures so deeply
imprest on his mind, and so they will call forth
smiles with not a grain of kindness in them.

"It certainly was not intended to confine the
pupil to a stereotyped copy which, if carried
out, would paralyze all his natural grace. His
initiation should be gradual.

"The best way would be to encourage the
child's natural gestures by making him recite
such pieces as describe the very simple events
of his own life. Let him speak about his plays,
describe a party in the country, a fête, etc.

"And when the child is reciting, the atten-
tive teacher should only correct him for his
faults of speech, and for making uncouth gestures which he may have overlooked; allowing
him when delivering his recitation to retain all

his naïve characteristics, or spontaneous enthusiasm.

"We must remember these three great causes which produce harmony of gesture and of speech ; *thought, feeling,* the *expression of the idea.*

"Children destined to lead a public life find as they grow older that they are very greatly assisted in their career by observing these three precepts; others, in consequence of having followed them, experience a happiness that by degrees extends to every one round them.

"If these rules be followed they will prevent timidity, which as we have seen often originates in a 'prime cause' that no amount of energy can crush."

What would not many mothers of our own day give to read these truths!

It might, perhaps, preserve us from listening to a prodigy eight years of age recite verses of Sully-Prudhomme, accompanying them with gestures like those of a broken doll, and whom we encore through courtesy.

In turning over the leaves that treat of estheticism in its relation to timidity we still find psychological reflections which are so appropriate to every age and country that we can not resist the temptation of citing them.

III.7

"Nearly all nationalities are inspired by seeing symbolic dancing, which is occasionally religious, but oftener sensual, and sometimes warlike in character.

"Shall we agree with the savants who sought the origin of this sentiment—which is only apparent in the human race—by saying that the art of dancing is a valuable adjunct in perpetuating the human race?

"Shall we not rather view it as a striving to express the beautiful in a tangible form leading one toward the highest ideals?

"By this means the soul is elevated and the most unfortunate can experience joys which can not be purchased with gold.

"A timid person can not enjoy the pleasures of dancing, for he becomes frightened and covered with confusion when he thinks any one is going to look at him."

This remark, which was true so many centuries ago, can be also applied to our modern life.

In dancing we must not only make up our minds that many eyes are riveted on us, but we must dance often, that is, attend balls, which requires a knowledge of the forms of society the practise of which tends to frighten the timid person.

He must be willing to enter society, to be introduced, to know how to ask a lady to dance, to dance gracefully, and to converse while resting between the dances.

It is also necessary for him to think where he is going so as not to collide with the other dancers; but should he knock against any one he ought to take the blame on himself, and make his excuses in a courteous and becoming manner.

And it is impossible for a timid man to do this.

It is the same with a musician who, when timid, feels his fingers contract, and the instrument being played with a stiff touch emits only a short and often a false tone, for his hands tremble.

Others are endowed with a voice, but they can never sing if they think any one is listening.

They at once become the prey of physical changes due to timidity, their throat contracts until they can not emit a sound, and if they do succeed their voice will have lost the purity and fulness that charmed us.

Reading further we come across the following reflections:

"Even in the art of painting natural objects the timid are at a disadvantage.

"They rarely attempt to reproduce the charming things they see in their dreams. They are satisfied with very commonplace subjects, unless they make a worthless choice leading them to outdo themselves by producing something quite extravagant.

"These erratic productions begin by merely being original, but by degrees—having been subjected to the distorted ideas of the timid artist, for he 'dare' not ask advice as he only takes counsel with himself—he entertains illusions regarding the faults of his work, until his productions become extremely eccentric, so he still thinks himself merely unconventional."

Many physiologists go so far as to say that art in the spring and fall exhibitions, which is quite beyond the comprehension of any one, is the work of the timid. People inquire why one artist paints women without faces, and why another paints flesh a beautiful sky-blue, and persons with impossible contours.

"Specialists," says Yoritomo, "need not look far for the answer, for these are the works of the timid; they were begun in a sensible way but gradually modified by the lonely artist's touch until they display these faults which the artist does *not perceive*."

Furthermore, we can readily see for ourselves how this all came about, when we look at the engravings of ancient costumes.

It seems impossible for us to imagine that our fathers and mothers could have appeared, and even been attractive in such absurd clothes. But should the caprice of fashion decree the return of these styles we would at first be greatly surprized, but soon growing accustomed to them we would not only tolerate them but admire them, and adopt them.

This lesson on estheticism in relation to the fault which is the subject of this book would not be complete without citing a few reflections of Shogun, on an especially painful subject. Timidity arises from being conscious of having a fault we can not hide.

"This is the only case," says he, "where it can conceal a refined soul.

"The confusion originates in a characteristic dread of offending others with the sight of his deformity.

"This fear is readily transformed into a wish that these disadvantages be forgotten through his developing rare talents.

"Have we not seen deformed men **charm** people with their poetry and their song!

"Is it necessary to possess a form like a beautiful statue in order to paint marvelously beautiful birds in a dreamy landscape?

"Does he who listens to the poems and the songs, and who admires the landscape, finding himself in an enchanted world, does he think of the deformity of the artist who was able to procure him those moments of exquisite joy.

"It is not of bodily defects we should be ashamed, but for those of the soul we should blush.

"If the soul be pure the face, no matter how unprepossessing it may be, will reflect its beauty.

"Have we not in troublous times seen men renowned for their ugliness inspire the people by their words, and dominate the minds of a crowd so thoroughly that it seemed but one soul vibrating in unison with his.

"At such a moment who would notice the man's face, except as it reflected the lofty sentiments which animated him!

"Sincerity, self-confidence, high-spirited audacity that conceives and executes great projects, contain harmonies that will always move us, in spite of bodily deformity, for the union of these qualities constitutes beauty."

LESSON VIII

TIMIDITY AND BUSINESS

YORITOMO lays special stress on the following axiom:

"Timidity is the stumbling-block to him who would seek his fortune in any line of work.

"It is always inauspicious, and in spite of his efforts—which rarely amount to anything because they are intermittent and unskilfully directed—the timid person will always see his fault loom up between him and success.

"On meeting strangers, he is liable to be disturbed by a feeling of fear mingled with shame, and if this be not fought against it will grow so strong as to become an insurmountable barrier.

"The fear of the recurrence of something that has caused him to suffer is a more potent factor than weakness of will. For the life of a man trying to rise above his environment is made up of perseverance and well-directed effort.

"Persons afflicted with this defect are never equal to making a sustained effort, for the horror they feel at the thought of going to the front precludes their taking any but the most necessary steps.

"They never make up their minds until the last moment, and they become discouraged if their first efforts are not crowned with success.

"Activity requires an initiative which at times may seem audacious, by giving the man confidence in himself, and in making him determined to force other people to have a corresponding confidence in him.

Speaking of perseverance, this includes militant realism, and prolific idealism.

Persistent efforts toward a desired goal smoothe the difficulties in the path.

"If a man about to undertake a hazardous journey were to neglect to supply himself with gold, and also with food, he would be in danger of giving out before reaching his destination," says the venerable sage, who adds:

"There are two qualities necessary in traveling through life: perseverance comes first, and then the energy to practise perseverance.

"A journey is only accomplished by taking one step after another, each step covering but the most infinitesimal part of the road to be traveled. It is the repetition of these steps, in

other words the continuous effort which enables
us to accomplish the roughest journey.

"One of the greatest stumbling-blocks to the
timid in the practical affairs of life is the difficulty he finds in expressing and upholding his
opinions.

"He is so unaccustomed to this that he thinks
he is in purgatory when trying to convince an
incredulous person or an adversary. Then the
fleeting impressions, so characteristic of weak
mentalities, prevent him from fixing his attention, and this, furthered by his habitual embarrassment, discomfits him, and so he ceases to
struggle.

"His faltering will prevents him from stating
facts graphically, so he describes them in a dull
and pointless way not calculated to convince
any one.

"If obliged to defend his views, he becomes
nonplussed at the slightest argument brought
forward by his adversaries. Unexpected objections confuse him so much that he loses all
confidence in his own judgment.

"If he attempt to persevere, the result is
usually disastrous, for as the timid can not co-
ordinate their ideas, they can not muster all
the facts they want to narrate.

"They soon become so embarrassed that they blush, which is especially annoying to them because they know what a bad effect it will have on their speech, and so they become more confused than ever.

"They are so nonplussed that they forget their best arguments, or even should they be able to recall them, they are so confused and so illy sustained as to be worthless."

These observations, so true in those days, are even more so to-day.

The world does not belong to the humble or to the weak; an intriguing schemer can very readily get the better of the timid. This is well proved by this little tale from far-off Japan, which brings to our mind many similar stories enacted in the Parisian world of intrigue.

"In a small province there dwelt a man who was extremely timid; his fault having separated him from his fellow men, he lived in the greatest seclusion.

"But as every one must have some pleasure, he cultivated chrysanthemums, celebrated for their beauty.

"The aspirations of his soul were satisfied in producing these superb flowers. Shunning contact with people, he took pleasure in contemplating the flowers, which filled the place of family to him. He spoke to them, admired them, fondled them without dread of becoming embarrassed, as he was when in the presence of people, and so experienced a tenderness akin to gratitude toward his beloved plants.

"One day he saw that a profane hand had devastated his garden; the most beautiful chrysanthemums, the peculiar and splendid appearance of which had given him the greatest pleasure, had been cut off their stems—they had been stolen.

"The lonely man, as we can readily imagine, was very much troubled, and terrified at the dilemma in which he was placed.

"Should he let the thief go unpunished, or take the necessary means to catch him, and have him arrested?

"What a struggle this was for him! But he loved the plants so dearly, and was so indignant that he determined to make the attempt; so, at night the amateur detective being very angry, mustered up sufficient energy to arrest the thief, and have him taken before the judge.

"He was not afraid of appearing in court, for he made sure of himself by learning almost verbatum the simple words he had to say.

"For example:

" 'I surprized this man as he was devastating my garden-border where my most beautiful chrysanthemums were in bloom.'

"But what was his astonishment when the thief turned on him and cried:

" 'They were not flowers, they were mallows.'

"Any one except a timid man would have used this reply as a means of making the thief confess.

"But he was so confused that he thought of no other course to take except to protest.

" 'They are flowers,' said he. 'They are mallows,' replied the malefactor; and he persisted, so that the proprietor, on being questioned by the judge, ended by saying in a stammering manner, that the flower and the mallow . . . , well, the mallow flower . . . , the purple flower——'

"This had the effect of making the judge lose patience, and he sent him back to his garden, after reprimanding him and reproaching him for having arrested an honest man without having any definite idea what accusation he wished to make against him."

This Japanese tale is absolutely true.

The timid person often has such a dread of contention that he prefers rather to agree with his adversaries than to stand up for his rights.

This feeling of embarrassment makes him loth to take the steps necessary to attain any profession; besides the calls he must make on his superiors, and the obligations of his profession, forcing him to come to the front, there are also other things he must observe.

There are visits of congratulation, of condolence, formal visits, visits prompted by curiosity, political visits, visits of introduction, etc., etc.

The last are especially trying to the timid who, no matter how high an opinion they have of their own worth, are haunted by the fear of appearing in a bad light.

They know very well that they can never find the word they want to use, and that their embarrassment will create an unfavorable impression.

On account of their lack of "sociability" they are unable to understand the difference between an ordinary solicitor, and one who feels authorized to remind his superiors that he would be glad to devote himself to the cause he serves.

In their dealings with their inferiors, the timid are always constrained, and in many instances they are duped.

They are ashamed to offer an employee reasonable wages; or having offered the usual amount, and the men demand excessive pay, they dare not dispute it.

To stand up for their rights would crush them completely and so the insolence of the debtor would always guarantee him against the solicitations of the timid.

They are a ready prey for base speculation, and for arbitrary demands; this is illustrated by an anecdote told by the savant, Hong-Loo.

"The savant, Hong-Loo," says Yoritomo, "was such a timid man that he did not sign his name to his principal works.

It was only by concealing his identity that he had sufficient courage to set forth his great precepts, so much appreciated by his contemporaries.

"But the cultivation of science was not of much use to Hong-Loo, for one day when he took time to look round him, he saw that his servants, having become tired of being fed on the words of the master, had left him, and that it was imperative for him to procure some money.

"For a long while usurers had taken advantage of his timidity and ignorance of the world,

and, when necessary, had lent him sums of
money for which they had reimbursed themselves by claiming a hundred times the value in
property.

"Therefore, he went to one of them and explained his predicament, blushing as he did so.

"The usurer protested; he said he was ruined,
that if he were murdered no available gold or
silver would be found. Nevertheless, . . . as
soon as Hong-Loo, who had become more confused than ever, began to speak, the man fas-
tened his eyes on the coat of the savant which
was made of beautiful blue satin with large
ibis embroidered in gold.

" 'Listen,' said he, 'my kind heart always gets
the better of me. I will not leave you in such
a predicament. I will give you ten gold pieces,
as a present, for you no longer own any land
or possessions.'

" 'Oh! my friend how kind of you!'

" 'Give me your coat.'

" 'But I shall not look fit to go out.'

" 'I will give you another in its place.'

"And he opened a lacquer chest and took out
a very old garment.

"The savant could scarcely refrain from
showing his displeasure. But as his case was

urgent, and his timidity made him afraid to argue over it, he accepted the situation, and exchanged his beautiful garment embroidered in gold, for this filthy rag, then extending his hand, but nothing was put in it.

" 'Before proceeding,' said the usurer, 'let us go over our accounts. I will buy your coat for ten pieces of gold which you are to return to me in thirty days, plus the interest. For the coat I have just sold you I am satisfied to take one piece of gold. Therefore, you owe me fourteen pieces of gold at new moon.

"Hong-Loo acquiesced.

" 'What resources have you with which to pay me? Let me tell you once more that you have not one piece of land left.'

"The poor man stammered out a few confused words.

" 'There, you see,' said the rapacious man, 'you don't know; well then, at the date fixt, I have the right to go to your house bringing with me officers of the law, and seize your manuscripts, for you possess nothing else. Would it not be wiser, now that you have the money, thanks to me, to pay me a portion of this debt?'

"The savant was about to object, but the usurer began again:

" 'Well now, it is all settled, I will keep the ten pieces of gold, and for the four still due me I will give you two hundred days' time.'

"And he pushed the poor Hong-Loo, who dared not reply, toward the door. All the way home he said to himself, 'It is strange! I have no money, I have lost my beautiful coat, I have contracted a debt . . . and it is legitimate too.' "

This graphic portrayal of a timid man strikes us by its simplicity.

Even if he be not always duped in such a simple manner, he is no less at the mercy of every schemer who speculates on his making but a show of defense.

These observations, so true in every respect, are equally applicable to all those who are obliged to count on the assistance of others in gaining their livelihood.

"The small tradesman," says the philosopher, "the most miserable man who carries the palanquin, as well as the most successful manufacturer; the poor clerk who passes his days printing characters with his brush, as well as the man whose birth has placed him on a throne, should all cultivate a polite manner, and the freedom of thought which tends to develop in

III.8

them the good qualities belonging to their sphere of life.

"If the small tradesman finds himself embarrassed on account of his timidity, he can not compete successfully with his neighbor whose persuasiveness attracts all the customers.

"If the successful manufacturer be overwhelmed with confusion when he should defend his interests, or when he wants to carry a point, his competitors will soon outstrip him, and he who is unprogressive is liable to be defeated.

"As for small clerks, if they do not distinguish themselves by doing something that requires intelligence, or by having ideas and presenting them in an attractive form, they will probably die as poor as they lived.

"Not only the high dignitary has to contend against smiling duplicity and polite audacity in order to keep control of the situation.

"The rivalry surrounding thrones makes it necessary for him who would maintain his authority to maintain it by means of energy concealed under an amiable exterior, so as to gain people's good-will, which might, at any time, become a power in the hands of those who know how to elicit it."

All timid persons have the fault of wanting

to put off making decisions, or doing tasks until to-morrow.

They do not always keep faith with themselves, but the fact of having deferred taking a step satisfies them for the time being.

Besides, resolutions put off from time to time seem less appalling, but the next day innumerable excuses present themselves and they are put off until the following day.

In business, this failing is one of the most frequent causes of failure.

Things constantly put off not only stand a great chance of never being accomplished, but the delinquents, always holding back, strike against closed doors, and see the business transacted without their assistance.

But the very thought of having to decide anything makes them so miserable that they can not make up their minds to it.

As soon as they work out a problem, a crowd of objections rise up in their feeble minds. If they take an opposite course, the obstacles that recently frightened them seem of very little consequence, but to offset this they consider the reasons in favor of the new project very inconsistent, now that it is a question of adopting them.

If they revert to their first opinion they experience the same feeling, for their hatred of accomplishing results precludes their considering any reasons except those which are opposed to carrying out the point in question.

And therefore, beaten about by most contrary desires, they permit themselves to entertain groundless hopes, which they reject as readily as they admit them.

When this struggle can no longer be maintained in the mind alone, when it must result in a decision, the timid person suffers more than ever.

He makes a tremendous effort for him, trying to express all the vague ideas that haunt him.

It is then that we see him entangling himself in phrases he is unable to finish, because the thought behind them has not assumed a definite form.

His words, following his thoughts, are inappropriate and disconnected.

He hesitates at every word, pronounces one or two syllables then seeing that it does not fit his thought, he does not finish it, but puts another word, which he considers more appropriate, in its place, only to thrust it aside before pronouncing it.

But the ideas he wishes to convey are so indistinct, and especially so diverse, that, owing
to lack of the power of concentration, he can
not grasp them firmly enough to express them
clearly.

He becomes more and more discouraged until
he accedes to everything his adversary wishes,
preferring to abandon the suit rather than to
be forced to contest it.

There have been instances of men holding
offices of public trust being so hampered by
timidity, which prevented them from entering
into any debate, that they abandoned their post
and retired before their time expired.

With few exceptions they sank into a dis-
graceful apathy, becoming hopelessly incapaci-
tated, and burying the few energetic impulses
which might have brightened their lives.

According to the teachings of Yoritomo, the
timid are prevented from giving alms tho they
would like to.

"Many people have been blamed," says he,
"for never having done a generous act because
they were restrained by bashfulness.

"Many people have borne the reputation of
being hard-hearted because they were judged
by appearances, whereas they were simply timid

persons who were disconcerted at the mere thought of being talked about.

"It is the sins of omission we must charge against those afflicted with this defect; the thought of speaking out, even if they have an important fact to announce, is so distressing that they prefer to suffer the disastrous consequences of a culpable silence.

"I knew of a family in modest circumstances being plunged in misery in consequence of one of these omissions.

"The son who was their support, a young man who was extremely timid, was in the employ of a rich *daimio*.

"One day when he was returning home from the palace, he heard a crackling sound; the library in which he worked was on fire.

"His first thought was to seek aid, and so he ran into the hall.

"The *daimio* who was coming from the opposite direction, and with whom he nearly collided, stopt him, and spoke so rudely to him that he was plunged in the deepest distress.

"He attempted to excuse himself by explaining his sudden entrance, but his throat muscles were so rigid that he could not utter a sound; his mouth was so parched that he could not speak a word, and so he stood there blushing, disgraced, and trembling.

"The *daimio*, attributing his embarrassment to the reprimand, shrugged his shoulders and passed by.

"The poor boy wished to tell some one in the palace about the fire, but how could he explain his silence when in the presence of his master?

"He made up his mind to confide in the elderly head-servant who had always been very kind to him, and so he went to look for him.

"When he had found him and had told him about it, some time had elapsed, and priceless manuscripts and rare collections had been devoured by the flames.

"The *daimio* was very angry, and dismissed him, and he and his family were obliged to drag out a miserable existence; whereas, if he had been able to conquer his attack of timidity, he would doubtless have been praised and well rewarded."

One of the usual effects of timidity is to encourage egotism.

Altho it is well, in the ordinary affairs of life, not to sacrifice oneself unnecessarily, it is unwise to ignore the power of generosity.

Those with whom we are too proud to shake

hands disdain us when we need their support.

"Here is another reason," says the Japanese savant, "for uprooting timidity.

"A timid person," he says, "is always egotistical, his fault making him so.

"He is too much occupied with himself to pay attention to the outside world.

"His sensations, his emotions, his judgment, are all subservient to his chief concern; the opinion of others.

"The timid men often really attribute their shyness to modesty, and lay undisputed claim to a crown, for the world belongs to those who are able to conquer it, and they look upon the timid, provided they are imprisoned in their timidity, as one adversary less to combat.

"A dupe of himself and his sentiments, the timid man gradually takes up his abode in the kingdom of impressions; thrust aside by the ambitious, who distrust him, deserted by people of deep reasoning powers, whom his attitude has displeased, he is obliged to lead a mediocre existence that will bring him neither the fortune nor the glory that he had not the ability to win.

"And from the depths of the solitude in which he is plunged, he detests humanity, whose charm he has never discovered."

LESSON IX

IN PRAISE OF AUDACITY

"Some virtues are separated from vices by a line so indistinct," says the learned old Japanese, "that few people can see it clearly, therefore they do not comprehend them, and so do not practise them.

"It is the duty of him who makes a specialty of cultivating minds, to enlarge the scope of generous impulses, and to teach the most humble to practise these virtues which until now have been reserved for the chosen few.

"Men who view things superficially rarely know the difference between pride and vanity, perseverance and obstinacy; economy and avarice, etc., etc.

"It is the same in regard to audacity, when it does not degenerate into boastfulness, for it ought also to be considered as one of the virtues that march at the head of the wonderful cortège led by energy.

135

"There is a Japanese axiom which says:

" 'The audacious will erect his palace on the bones of effrontery.'

"In order to define the boundaries, so easy to step over, which separate audacity from effrontery and presumption, one must first define audacity in the best sense of the word.

"This virtue is the exclusive attribute of the strong; it includes the union of essential qualities that form a solid and unassailable phalanx."

It requires, as we have already said, energy, but especially will-power.

These two qualities, which the ordinary person usually confounds, are so distinct that it is impossible to lack the one while possessing the other.

Will is a powerful quality by which we gain the force to make decisions, and to carry them out.

Energy consists in a steady will, originating in a determination to maintain it.

Energy, issue of the will, completes it, in the sense that it makes it tenacious, by the help of vigor and firmness.

The will determines decisions, but energy chooses them, by teaching us how to concentrate our will on a definite point, and by making us

resolve not to deviate from the main path leading to it.

In a word: Will directs strength.

"The audacious," says the venerable Japanese, "are always courageous. There are many
kinds of courage, the most difficult to practise is
not always that one feels on the battlefield.

"Obscure courage, which calls for devotion
that is not perceived, and which, therefore, can
not claim any reward, is the most difficult to
maintain.

"But this quality is rarely possest by the
audacious who especially require a determined
will and the dash necessary to accomplish what
they have undertaken.

"There is another quality required by him
who would be audacious, and that is ambition.

"An error that can not be too strongly re-
futed is that of considering ambition as a fault.

"Ambition is indispensable to him who would
strive for honors, and for the highest advance-
ment.

"It is the lever which removes obstacles, the
talisman which opens the doors of the caverns
in which are the treasures hidden from the
timid.

"This is the path that must be taken by every

man who attempts to march toward the highest ideals, which result in his becoming well-nigh perfect.

"There is only one case when ambition can not be praised, and that is when it has baseness and cupidity for its aim.

"But debased minds are rarely capable of making sustained efforts, and the ambitious man should be gifted with judicious and persistent energy.

"The audacious have been reproached with being inclined to ruthlessly break through the obstacles that lay in their path.

"These objections can only be made by narrow-minded people who occupy themselves with details instead of looking at results.

"If the end in view be noble and carried out well, the good that will result to the many will give it such weight that any sacrifices made will not be regretted.

"Under no circumstances must audacity be confounded with temerity.

"The audacious excel in judging the relations of things and their consequent results.

"Rash people do not take into consideration conditions, and so they only see the end they are aiming for."

A few lines further on we find an anecdote illustrating this point, and displaying the delicate coloring which is one of the charms of the Japanese philosopher.

"Two men set out to seek Fortune.

"They traveled in vain over hill and dale, for they could not find a trace of the capricious goddess.

"They were beginning to despair, when, one evening, just as the sun was setting amid rose-colored clouds, they reached the edge of a swamp that seemed to shut off their path.

"On the opposite side green lawns and blossoming trees tempted them.

"In vain they sought a way to reach these, but the deep marsh seemed the only connecting link.

"They did not dare to attempt to cross the marsh, for they knew they would sink in the quicksand. So they tried to avoid retracing their steps by finding another route, when a form was outlined in the brilliant sky. It was she, there could be no doubt, it was Fortune, smiling and beckoning them to come to her.

"Trembling with emotion, they stood still a moment gazing at the woman who was urging them to join her.

"She was walking along the border of the swamp.

" 'Do you see her?' said one of them.

" 'Yes,' replied his friend, 'let us go toward her.'

" 'But how can we?'

" 'By taking the shortest route'; he cried, as he dashed forward.

" 'Have you lost your senses,' said his companion as he tried to restrain him. 'You know very well that these marshes engulf every one foolhardy enough to attempt to enter them.'

" 'What do I care? I must reach Fortune no matter how.'

" 'What good will it do us if we lose our lives? Rather help me to cut down the branches of these trees that obstruct our way.'

" 'And suppose she should disappear?'

" 'That would serve us right for running after her.'

"But the timorous man would not listen further, so he broke loose from his friend and plunged into the marsh which engulfed him as its prey.

"While this was going on, the other man broke off boughs and threw them on top of the muddy surface, entwining them carefully.

"He risked his life, of course, but he did not go to certain death like his companion, and when he realized the danger he suddenly sprang forward, and without being alarmed at the cracking of the branches behind him, as they disappeared in the muddy marsh, he made a few strides which brought him to the opposite bank.

"Fortune had continued to smile since the attempt made by the rash man, and now she stopt a moment, for she was interested in the efforts made by the audacious man, who was dextrous enough to seize her, before she vanished, by catching hold of the tail of her coat."

The difference between the audacious man and the rash man is summed up in this fable.

Of course, conditions are not always favorable for the work the audacious person undertakes, for in that case he would not merit the name; but he does not hesitate to enter the lists, provided he thinks these conditions supported by a foundation sufficiently solid to ensure the success of an undertaking requiring intelligent audacity and reflection.

For as soon as he weighs the result of his acts, he will proceed bravely and nobly, and enter confidently into the struggle for which he feels himself fully prepared.

The audacious have been blamed for cultivating a high opinion of themselves, which in
these modern days we call egotism. If to discern one's good qualities and to acknowledge
them be a sign of egotism, the audacious man is
surely an adept, for he has not the slightest
inclination to make sacrifices that no one will
see; he wishes to succeed, and he walks straight
ahead, his eyes fixt on the goal—success.

This is illustrated by the following proof,
which we cull from the rich collection of fables
by Yoritomo.

"In the days when enchanters disdained to
come to the assistance of mortals, one of them
had a gigantic ladder made, the last step of
which touched the threshold of the palace of
universal knowledge.

"Not all who were called were chosen; some,
after mounting a few steps, stopt to enjoy the
shelter offered them by second-rate acquaintances; others got as far as the porch, where
philosophers and savants were awaiting them,
under lofty colonnades.

"Very few of them set foot on the last step;
for that rung of the ladder, being uneven, required very steady nerves to mount and fur-
nished nothing to lean against. Besides, the

precipices which they had ascended were strewn
with the corpses of those who had stumbled on
the way up.

"These were the rash people who had attempted the ascent without first curing themselves of vertigo.

"But the audacious, who were prepared by
having been accustomed to energetic action,
both mental and physical, those who had learned
to master themselves before attempting to set
out to conquer universal knowledge, those whose
moral strength was sufficient to safeguard
against vertigo produced by the height, by
giving them the wished-for strength to keep
their eyes fixt on heaven, those, and those alone,
were able to take a place along side of the elect.
Besides, on reaching the last step, they were re-
ceived by men who possest the secrets of eternity,
and who initiated them into the mysteries, and
transformed them into beings almost divine."

The audacious person, then, is he who can
march straight to the goal braving the dangers,
which he has well weighed.

He never permits himself to be swayed by
fancies; he only undertakes enterprises that are
sufficiently definite to attract a man of his
resolute character.
III.9

"He who only judges life through his dreams," says Yoritomo, "is most likely to remain deceived forever, for he will never be able to tell the right road."

The audacious person is always in a hurry, and when occupied, his attention is never distracted by what he sees on the road.

He either disdains, or overcomes the obstacles in his path, and marches forward to the highest ideals, his mind filled with this thought: "One must be daring; the world belongs to the audacious."

LESSON X

THE ACQUISITION OF POISE

WHEN we reflect on all the inconveniences of timidity, from the usual tedium of every-day life to the gravest consequences it entails, we experience the same feeling as when looking at a sick person—we wish to cure him, or at least to help him.

Is timidity a curable disease?

"Without a doubt," says Yoritomo; "and in order to accomplish this readily, it is simply necessary that the timid person submit to a mental treatment, which will at first not have much effect, but by degrees the improvement will become more marked in his mental state, in his way of looking at things, and in the strength of his resolutions.

"Let us first discuss the mental state. The timid man, as we have seen, is at times too frightened to speak, then again he is consumed by shame, or so puffed up with self-sufficiency that he imagines every gesture he makes is being commented on.

145

"He is so greatly influenced by his thoughts that his lonely reflections insensibly assume forms quite different from those of the initial stage.

"If he perceive the incredulity he calls forth when stating his theories, he becomes embarrassed. This lack of reasoning power often lets him indulge in exaggerated statements, which make people doubt him still more, until they become convinced that the contrary of what he says is the truth; this makes him more angry than ever, and he involuntarily resorts to lies.

"He is often unjust in consequence of the inclination we all have to make others suffer the results of our own faults.

"In order to remedy this, the timid man should make every effort to gain energy, which permits concentration; not the injurious kind of concentration which he has exercised up to the present time, but the self-examination which will enable him to recall the events of the day, without enlarging on them, or omitting anything regarding them.

"He should then use his best efforts to make this investigation in the most conscientious manner.

"By this means, he will gradually become

familiar with the qualities that are, in a way, the beginning of energy.

"If his thoughts wander during this time, he must grasp them again firmly, and take up the chain of his memory of the daily events at the very place where he dropt it.

"This exercise is indispensable in curing the timid man, for in the course of these recollections he would find twenty causes to confuse him, or to make him angry with himself.

"For twenty or thirty days he should attempt nothing, besides concentrating his attention as quickly and as carefully as possible.

"His first care, during this initial period, should be to review what happened, day by day, and this he should do more and more minutely.

"For this, a reclining position, or an easy, comfortable position requiring no thought, is advisable.   Then he must close his eyes and relax his entire body.

"That done, he should recall the incidents of the day, exercising his will-power more and more by trying not to deviate into reveries which would interrupt his train of thought.

"He who succeeds in this is on the road to recovery; he can now attack the other part of his task.

"After having carefully recalled all the events of a day, he should consider them in relation to the fault he is trying to overcome.

"If, for example, he finds that he had remained silent when hearing a compliment, or a remark to which he should have replied, let him prepare the reply just as tho he were going to make it, and repeat it over several times, trying to speak slowly and without stammering.

"If, on the contrary, he exaggerate unduly, he should question himself secretly, and by disengaging his personality from his judgment, he should look at his statements through the eyes of a stranger.

"Many times during this introspection he will feel confused, as he calmly reviews the ridiculous appearance he made.

"But, instead of despairing, and conceiving an aversion for the world, he should arm himself with a firm resolve to avoid the repetition of similar faults.

"This determination is the culminating point in curing timidity and is just what we find most difficulty in getting him to do.

"In fact, he never could have made up his mind to it if he had not been prepared through practising the first exercise for concentration.

"The thirty or forty days in which his attention shall have been rigorously trained every evening will have gained him the power of co-ordination, which, hitherto, he has not been able to exercise.

"During this time the effort he had made to classify the little daily happenings, and to concentrate his attention on them, without letting his thoughts wander, will have slowly unfolded the centers of energy in his brain, of which, as yet, he is not conscious, but which are there ready to act.

"This is the reason it is indispensable to continue to practise the first part of the cure for timidity, until the defect be overcome completely. It would be very unwise to shorten or to omit this.

"When consoled by the thought of finding himself able to regulate his thoughts, he will see that he is no longer a slave to his mental weakness, and it will be easier for him to resolve to be on his guard hereafter.

"To accomplish this, he should, after having recalled the phases of his presumption, renew them, but in modified and appropriate form.

"He should try to remember, as well as he can, and word for word, the exaggerated thoughts he exprest, repeating them aloud, not this time the sentences he intended to say, but those he did actually speak, in order to convince himself of their childishness.

"When that is accomplished, he should resort to introspection, and replace his fantastic ideas —which he had held to most obstinately—by formulas appropriate to the occasion, and so strike a middle course.

"He should repeat these sentences, if possible, word for word, and endeavor to speak them before witnesses.

"Then he should think of the occasions in which he might be placed in analogous situations, and should prepare replies to the questions he thinks might be discust.

"He ought to speak these replies out loud, trying to articulate every syllable distinctly, and to guard against stammering.

"At last he will make a resolve not to indulge in grotesque fancies, but, instead, to take a calm view of the objections made by those with whom he is arguing.

"Besides, these objections will be made less frequently, because his words will be more temperate, and his attitude calmer.

"In order to prove the strength of his resolutions, he should set himself a task. For example, to call on such and such a person the following day, and salute him by following a formula he had carefully thought out.

"It is well, if possible, to select some one accustomed to giving large receptions, for the exchange of sentiments will thus be curtailed, and it will be easier for the timid man to recite the sentences he has learned, if he knows that the ordeal will soon be over.

"If, on reviewing his conduct, he finds that he has been very irritable, he should, on the following day—after having thoroughly investigated the cause of his anger, and realizing its childishness—revive this incident which caused him annoyance, so as to be able to master it if he feels it likely to crop out again.

"Or if, as most frequently happens, the embarrassment that disconcerted him was caused by blushing at an inopportune time, he should recall the events which caused him to blush, speak aloud the words that brought it on, and familiarize himself, as best he can, with the incident that caused it.

"The best way to do this is to speak unreservedly of it, even if this allusion to it make him blush all the more.

"In this case, instead of making a cowardly reply, he should face the enemy, and when he has ceased blushing he ought to continue to converse on the same subject, or even bring it up again, should the conversation have taken another turn, and keep this up until he blushes but slightly, or not at all.

"The timid have great difficulty in seeing things in their proper focus.

"We can not repeat too often that it is in solitude thoughts are changed beyond recognition.

"It is very difficult to prevent this metamorphosis of the original thought, if the timid person keep his reflections to himself. Therefore, it is well for him to communicate them to others. However, he should take good care not to stand up for them if he sees an expression of astonishment on the faces of those with whom he is talking.

"In this case, the best way is for him to go back to the formation of the idea in order to compare it with what it has developed into, tracing its slightest variations.

"This is incontestable evidence which the afflicted man alone can furnish, and which he can fully control, provided he prepare himself by practising the first exercise.

"As to steadiness of purpose, that can only be attained gradually, and so, tho the timid man often slide backward, he should, in the daily review of his life, not fail to take note of his triumphs, which will greatly encourage him.

"There is such a thing as anticipating timidity, that is to say simply apprehending it, but which is quelled by reason in the moment for action.

"The timid man, while being cured, is distrest by the thought that he has to accomplish some deed, or take a certain step, but his reason strengthened by his custom of daily introspection enables him to judge his actions, so that he can resist this inclination.

"Of course he will still suffer, but as he no longer secretes himself, he will gradually be able to get rid of this apprehension when he realizes how absurd it is.

"Indeed, the anguish experienced by the timid is mostly the result of the fear of being defeated, and he can not free himself from this anxiety, except by proving to his own satisfaction on what a slight foundation it rests.

"After having gained this victory over his mind, he should give his attention to his defects, that is to say, awkwardness, uneasiness of mind, stammering, and lack of tact, which especially need to be conquered, as these defects confuse the timid man so that he takes refuge in isolating himself, fearing to meet renewed affronts.

"Therefore, it is well for him to realize the necessity for these outward manifestations. For example, if he ought to be present at a meeting, it would be well for him to think of it for some time beforehand, according to the rule that the repetition of an emotion engenders the habit of feeling it, and this habit will dull the first impression, or cause it to disappear entirely.

. "Therefore, it is necessary that the timid man familiarize himself with the gestures he intends making, so that he can make them without effort.

"Now is the time to consider how to prevent him from suffering, as formerly, from these inconveniences.

"To cure awkwardness, he should practise walking gracefully, and coming forward without disgracing himself.

"This result can be accomplished by thinking of it frequently, if not constantly.

"He should practise carrying his head high and looking people square in the face; of course he should not maintain this position for any length of time, being unaccustomed to it, and it would be better for him to practise this exercise but a short time at first, gradually lengthening it.

"For the first few days he should accustom himself to assume this attitude during five minutes; three or four days later, he may try it again for ten minutes, then a quarter of an hour, and so forth.

"But, in order that this treatment be effective, the timid man should persevere in it, that is to say, if his resolution waver when doing his exercise, and he turn away his eyes before the bold gaze of a passer-by, if he neglect, even for a few seconds, to carry his head well, or to hold himself up straight, he should try over again, until he can maintain the attitude during the time he had determined.

"He should begin by practising addressing acquaintances on the street.

"At first he should only speak very short sentences, prepared in advance, and appropriate to every one, such as asking after health, and affairs in general. The stumbling-block of the timid is their lack of simplicity. This is very often caused by a wish to be complex, and this, inflicted on others, repulses them, as we have seen.

"These endeavors should be made quickly, for the rule is, to allow no time for embarrassment. And it is very necessary for the timid to feel that they have deported themselves creditably when interchanging compliments, thereby gaining courage to make another attempt.

"If the stammering recur, he should, on returning home, repeat the unfortunate phrase, at first slowly, then more rapidly, articulating fully, that is to say, by exaggerating the movements of his mouth and lips so that he can pronounce the words mechanically.

"But this is not all; he should not consider the victory complete if on the morrow, at the same hour, he has not sought a similar occasion to speak the same words to some person he meets.

"If he succeed he will have made double progress, for with one blow he will have conquered apprehension and a physical defect.

"Regarding awkwardness; it is necessary to correct it by taking great care, when alone, to practise repeating the actions we anticipate doing on the morrow.

"Thus, if he has calls to pay, he should practise entering his house as tho it were a stranger's. If he repeat over and over again the gestures he expects to make the following day, these gestures will become familiar to him, and he will make them in a natural manner when in public.

"He must be careful not to attempt anything complicated. Naturalness, hunted down by timidity, returns by degrees and forces it to yield.

"After these first steps the rest is easy, and the timid, being no longer the slave of a fault, may be allowed to give their attention to the faculties that lay dormant in their minds.

"Being no longer dominated by this fault which isolated them from the rest of the world, they may dream of attaining success; thus they would lose the habit of envying people.

"If this ferment still retain the old germs they should instantly be removed. The timid man who wishes to get rid of his humility, should exercise rigorous introspection, provided he really wants to be thoroughly cured."

If we were to write a commentary on the sage precepts of Shogun, it would be to advise those who really want to be cured, not only to take advice but to have an intelligent protector to sustain them, and to make them persevere on the difficult road of improvement.

First, the mere fact of confiding to a mind specialist would, in the timid, mean one step toward sociability; it would also act as a modifier in cases in which habit tends to make them transpose their first thought into a senseless proposition.

This will also be a great help by preparing the timid man to join in discussions in the future.

But one will ask, would it not be inconvenient to the timid to take refuge in the will of another instead of thinking for himself?

No, not if the mentor be a conscient and a wise man, for he will be able to inspire his pupil to rise above the effluence of his own will, and lead him to perceive the strength that he possesses.

The timid man may often be compared to a timorous man who trembles when in solitude, but is reassured if near a child too weak to assist him in any way.

The mere fact of feeling that there is some one by is sufficient to cause his chimeras, which haunt him when alone, to disappear.

There have been instances of timid persons having an unnatural dread of crossing open places, but they will cross them all alone, and of their own free will, if accompanied by a child who is under their protection.

As is the case with all the mentally deficient, the timid man feels he needs a support, no matter how frail, and this protection will be still more felt if it be extended by an influential man, whose kind indulgence will be a great help to him.

But it requires great tact to play the rôle of this mental healer, for if the tutelage be too apparent, it has a very bad influence on him he is trying to save.

On the contrary, he should liken his disease to a child learning to walk, who should at times be left alone, but who starts forth with confidence only when he has hold of a hand to prevent him from falling.

A child must have some liberty to awaken in him a feeling of responsibility, and make him talk, and if his mother never lets him out of her arms he becomes so accustomed to her protecting care that he meets with accidents whenever he ventures forth.

Let the timid man feel assured that, should he become confused, no one will ridicule him, and he will venture to speak out; and to overcome his inclination to be presumptuous, it is necessary to make him see things in their proper focus.

In this cure of timidity, requiring so much tact, it is the part of the doctor to take especial pains to induce his patient to cling to his resolutions which he is often unable to do, on account of lack of will-power.

The doctor must also prepare him by degrees for a complete change in his appearance and his views.

And he should especially try to avoid the recurrence of anything calculated to provoke worry and embarrassment, which precede these defeats.

If an incident of this kind occur the mentor should at once make light of it by persuading the patient that it was not noticed.

If he can pretend that he did not see it, he will lessen its importance, and also the chances of the patient's repeating it.

Yoritomo also gives his attention to the great care the man attempting to make the cure should take to gratify—without alarming his patient—the unacknowledged need of sympathy which all timid persons feel.

"If people are too demonstrative," says he, "they frighten him, so the confidence of the patient must be gained by degrees.

"He should be made to realize that he is supported by a firm and intelligent master, one who is indulgent, and who takes a flattering interest in him; for his mental seclusion has always prevented him from being communicative. Those persons who do not strive to become known through works or speeches are soon forgotten.

"The timid person is flattered to see that he is considered of some consequence, and he will gain confidence in himself when with any one able to make him think he understands him; so, by degrees, confidence increases between master and pupil, which results in opening the lips of the latter.

"If the doctor can inspire the timid man with confidence in his protection, and make him let out his pent-up energy, he will gradually seek the support of this force, which will slowly permeate him, and modify his condition almost before he knows it.

"Then the cure is easy, and all that has been said on this subject can be put in practise with good results.

"It can not be reiterated too often that one must persevere, notwithstanding the difficulties in the way.

"The timid person may, at times, be compared to the chrysalis of a butterfly, which, for lack of needed sunlight and care, perishes miserably in its ugly envelop, instead of charming us by its grace and brilliant coloring."

LESSON XI

THE RECOGNITION OF ONE'S WORTH

THE timid person, according to the teachings of Yoritomo, may, like many others, be cognizant of his worth, but, says he, "it is very rare that this conviction inspires him with a wish to correct his defect.

"Cognizance of his worth rarely produces in the timid any feeling but vanity.

"He considers it a reason why he should take refuge in his timidity, and disdainfully isolate himself because he feels that no one understands him.

"He thinks the opinions of others are very unjust; but he suffers less from this than one would imagine. There is a special kind of pride which causes him to congratulate himself on the amiable way he bears this lack of appreciation.

"This does not have to amount to humiliating him, in order to make him admire the stoicism with which he submits to these trials.

"His pride is certainly grafted on a great deal

of conceit, to which is added a thorough contempt for those who do not understand him.

"He does not realize that his being so uncommunicative, makes it difficult to give him the due credit for his knowledge and his intelligence.

"This kind of pride is, therefore, very undesirable. It is not the lofty sentiment, so elevating to our souls. It must be fought against for it gives to him who cultivates it the faculty of admiring himself when not at his best.

"Neither should we confound the noble feeling of recognizing our own worth, with vanity, or, worse still, with the worship of 'self,' which is the principal failing of the timid.

"If the timid man pride himself on bearing imaginary sorrows bravely, it is always because of his being so isolated and deprived of all intercourse with others, that his opinions regarding self-glorification are limited.

"This 'ego' of the timid becomes a god whose altar is his heart.

"It is there he takes refuge in hours of humiliation; and this creed is the source of the self-love which causes him to have an exaggerated opinion of his own worth, and to depreciate that of others.

"On the contrary, he who is cognizant of possessing good qualities which he stands ready to defend, regrets this tendency to admire oneself, and judges himself most impartially.

"He courts severe criticism, as a means of gaining a perfect knowledge of his aptitudes, and takes the easiest road to cultivate them.

"As he acknowledges his faults he profits by reproof, and he is willing to turn back, change his plans, or, if need be, the orientation of his energy, if he feel himself on a path leading nowhere.

"Instead of isolating himself, and draping himself in false dignity, he will—provided he be deeply imprest with his worth, and also that he recognize his faults—try to expand, by taking valuable advice.

"And he will discuss subjects calmly and quietly without giving way to the impressionability that makes the timid one-sided and stubborn.

"It is an acknowledged part that he who greatly overvalues, or undervalues himself can not expect to be successful. In the first case he is blinded by his self-sufficiency; in the second, he believes himself so inferior that he has not the courage to strive to excel.

"The best way of finding good material for making comparisons is to study those who have attained the first rank. The most powerful men usually have some defects of character, a fact which should serve to encourage men who have a just appreciation of their own worth.

"One should not forget that mistrust of oneself kills all initiative, and prevents one from accomplishing any kind of work, for one can not succeed in an enterprise if it be not undertaken with the conviction that it is going to be successful.

"If, on making certain comparisons, we feel assured that we have as great ability as those who have attained to brilliant positions, we should confidently make the attempt on which depends future success, in whatever form it presents itself.

"If, on the contrary, on examining ourselves impartially, we find that we have not so much knowledge as those whom we take for our models, far from being discouraged, we must, on the contrary, try to acquire these qualities, at the same time carefully fostering the advantages we have over those we emulate.

"And then, it is not necessary to imitate great men in order to become celebrated in our turn.

"On the contrary it is a good thing to preserve our personality, as well as our virtues, and
sometimes even slight defects, when well regu-
lated, may lead to success.

"Have all fruits the same flavor? Do they
all look alike?

"If some of them are rough, will that rough-
ness not serve to protect their hearts? And if
others are bitter, do they not enclose the sooth-
ing balm, the virtues of which are concealed by
the bitterness.

"It is most important to guard parents and
educators against the stupid custom of humiliating children before their faces, under pretence
of preventing them from being proud.

"When will we comprehend that pride, well
directed, may lead to the accomplishment of
great deeds that humility can never attain to.

"We do not refer here to the humility that
makes a great display, by exhibiting itself every-
where, for that is only another form of pride.
We are only discussing voluntary effacement
caused by distrusting oneself, which results in
those who yield to it, feeling themselves to be
inferior.

"We can not sufficiently blame people who
are bringing up children, for saying to them:

'You have no brains!' or, 'How ugly you are!'

"Even if it be true it makes the child emphasize his physical or mental defect.

"There are few people without some good points. Oftentimes the most ill-favored person has some one charm.

"Even those who have scarcely any intelligence frequently have one faculty developed out of all proportion to the others.

"It is this one charm, this one faculty which should be cultivated. If, however, the person be inclined to be vain a few discreet remarks may be made to the effect that in other ways he is far from perfect.

"Instead of saying to a child, 'How ugly you are!' provided it be the truth, we should try to keep him from noticing it, for the feeling that he is less favored than others may lead to an embarrassment engendered by the shame he experiences on becoming conscious of his inferiority.

"He who thinks himself 'ugly' has not the same poise as another when out in the world, and if he become envious, which is almost always inseparable from such an avowal, he will swell the list of the many timid persons afflicted with envy, whose grievances we have narrated.

"This mistaken method of preventing vanity is still even more culpable when aimed at the intellect.

"I knew a child whose mind—evidently not well trained—was atrophied by severe criticism.

"He was so weak that he could not be taught the principals of art, or of war, and he became utterly indifferent to everything, and somewhat suspicious. All his family noticed this.

"When wandering in the garden, he would hum to himself, and dream, and he would not apply himself to anything, so his family gave him up as a hopeless case.

"I became interested in him, especially as I saw that this young boy was a victim of the prejudice which endeavored to make people realize what they should be, by making them abject, in other words precluding them from making any efforts.

"I cultivated the boy's acquaintance, and, without frightening him, I induced him to speak. Our conversations were always very simple—the flowers in the garden, the butterflies, furnishing the subjects.

"One day I said to him.

"'As you are so fond of butterflies and flowers, why don't you read about them?'

"He gave me a frightened glance.

" 'I can't learn anything,' said he. 'My parents say it was "time lost trying to teach me anything, for I was too stupid to learn." '

" 'Would you like to try?'

" 'I don't know.'

"As he said this, a many-colored butterfly settled on a large lily; the child seized my hand.

" 'How beautiful it is!' said he, in wonder.

"Then I began to explain to him how the larva was transformed into the brilliant insect.

"The child listened in rapt attention.

"After some weeks of daily intercourse he told me that he was studying in books about the things I had told him. I encouraged him by praising his newly acquired knowledge, and I spoke of him, before his face, praising his attainments.

"This young boy who had been thrust aside gradually lost the feeling that he was insignificant, and so he willingly talked of what he had learned, and he heard the sweet sounds of praise.

"He became one of the most distinguished naturalists, and his parents, who once thought that he could accomplish nothing, are now proud of him.

"What was the cause of this metamorphosis? The realization of his own worth that I had inculcated in the little child who had been made to believe that he was a hopeless nonentity.

"This is a more difficult task when treating undeniable physical defects.

"Then it is that we should strive to develop the good qualities of the mind and sow the field with all kinds of knowledge, so that when the child grows to be a man he will be so cognizant of his intellectuality that he will not feel disturbed by his physical defects.

"It is always bad to hide from children the knowledge of their good points; there are cases in which this method—based on a narrow judgment—may become criminal.

"Was it not Shogun, who, nearer our own times, said that 'the sadness of him who is ignorant of the world is but the cowardice of him who despairs of success.'

"Why, then, close the door of the world to any human being, by refusing him its key; the recognition of his own worth."

LESSON XII

THE RIGHT ATTITUDE

AMONG the many remarks we have culled from the valuable works of Yoritomo, there is one which especially strikes us.

"The bearing of a person, even more than his face, is the index of his soul."

And he adds:

"That is why the movements of the timid are always *gauche,* indicating a lack of sincerity, which is one of their failings, for it is rarely that his words correspond to his thoughts.

"Freedom of thought alone gives ease of movement, which we value above everything.

"This grace of movement can never be attained by the timid, for the following reasons:

The gesture always precedes the speech, for it takes place when the impression is made.

"As this impression, in the case before us, is extremely mobile and unstable the movements expressing it would be discordant and disjointed.

"This is very apparent when listening to actors who have not perfected themselves in the fine points of their art.

"The words they speak merely voice a reflected sentiment, and they accent it by gestures which follow the words, instead of preceding them, as would be the case in real life.

"That explains the motions made by all timid persons.

"Can we say that a blustering manner is more nearly allied to the truth in that it is less constrained?

"By no means. He alone who can combine judicious reserve with self-mastery has sufficient control over himself to have sincere manners, which he will always retain, as they are natural to him.

"One must take especial care not to be wrecked on the shoals, well known to so many timid people, who, in order to avoid embarrassment when in public assume an extreme coldness of manner.

"They imagine that in this way they hide their emotions and escape the martyrdom of coming in contact with people.

"Some of them take refuge in a disdainful silence; they consider a mocking smile an easy way of replying to an argument. This behavior, which enables them to get their bearings, possesses the advantage of giving them time to think, and to form their sentences.

"By the time the sentence is painfully put together it is usually too late to speak it, the conversation having taken another turn; and the opportunity for making the remark that he has elaborated with so much care has long since passed by.

"For others, these different devices have but one advantage, which is that by employing them the timid can obviate reflection which, as their minds lack virility, is a slow process with them.

"The timid also feign gentleness, and they are obsequiously polite; they do not know how to make objections nor to banter and so they give their approval to everything, without exercising any judgment.

"These remarks apply especially to the humble; they live in perpetual dread of displeasing, and are disturbed by what others think of them.

"Are they more sincere? Certainly not, for their entire countenance indicates embarrassment and artifice.

"This timid person seems to be steeped in

humility, is often rebellious; the other one walks through life with head bent down and eyes lowered, and pities every one else for not living up to the ideals he has created, and to which he, himself, is not able to attain.

"But the timid will scarcely admit that to themselves, as in their inner life they are very audacious. They mistrust those who do not know the wonderful deeds of which they dream themselves capable.

"The bearing of the timorous is insincere. They are inclined to mysticism, not so much through conviction and striving after an ideal, as through fear of being punished in the next world.

"They lead a life like a rabbit, and everything which disturbs them, whether under the guise of pleasure or of grief, frightens them.

"As the rabbit fears the approach of the hunter, so they fear everything that can lead to an event in the piteous round of their days; and the slightest incident disturbs them greatly.

"They are always pessimistic, and they also have this peculiarity that they are but slightly affected by a great joy, but are dismayed at the least contrariety.

"It is very wrong to confound them with the

III.11

modest, who are one species in the order of beings devoid of energy.

"Modesty, the virtue wrongfully lauded by all writers, nevertheless possesses a great personal value, not usually recognized, and in that lies the blame. For the sake of the common good no one has the right to let the ability within him lie dormant.

"But the humble can not reproach themselves with this. If they are humble it is usually because they have no salient characteristics; their faculties are undeveloped and dull, as well as their minds and their persons, while their bearing reflects their inefficiency.

"Reserve, calmness, presence of mind, all these attributes of energy conscient of its force, are the qualities which should reflect in the bearing of him who possesses this virtue.

"Movements prompted by clear reasoning are always in harmony with the thoughts, and produce the poetry of motion which we value more than anything, especially because it reflects the soul.

"The strong man ought not to be too talkative, or too taciturn; too apathetic, or too turbulent; too obsequious, or too irascible.

"His conduct will be absolutely ruled by

giving things their proper weight. This virtue, which can only be attained by the energetic, will govern his thoughts, regulate his impulses and his movements, impressing one with the perfect harmony of his physical bearing, a veritable reflex of his mental attitude.''

As we read in the precepts of the venerable Shogun; the true bearing, which should be the objective point of every effort, is only the direct consequence of a sound soul manifesting itself externally.

It is the indelible mark by which one can recognize all the energetic, that is to say those who are freed from the shortcomings attributed to the timid and have undertaken this journey toward the highest development, an instance of which Yoritomo narrates in one of those epologs which he loves so well.

''Some men,'' says he, ''set out on a journey to a marvelous country. A large company had started, but after a few days the ranks thinned out. Some of them, the timorous, who were encumbered with a burden of useless scruples, succumbed under the weight of their burden.

''Others, the timid, were frightened by the difficulties they found in taking the initiative, always so painful to them.

"The modest, after a few days march, fell behind, fearing to be looked at, and people were already beginning to leave them to themselves.

"The apathetic, having grown weary, lay down in the ditches by the side of the road, and slowly ate the provisions they had brought for the journey, never thinking of the time later on when they might need them.

"The blusterers and the presumptuous, after having given way to the most ardent enthusiasm, had retreated at the first appearance of danger.

"The envious, instead of trying to emulate the courage of those at the head of the column, only tried to put obstacles in their way, over which they themselves were the first to stumble.

"Those who were rash were thinned out in consequence of their senseless imprudence.

"So that after some days only a ·handful reached Eden, the end of their route.

"And these men were the energetic, those to whom this virtue had given the audacity, ambition, cool-headedness, and self-mastery necessary to overcome the perils and, if need be, ward them off. Those whose calm and dignified demeanor had imprest their companions soon followed their example, the value of their procedure having profoundly imprest them."

The true bearing is then that which allows the exercise of tractable will, conqueror of timidity.

It originates always in a nobleness of soul which is its own recompense, for it is by this nobility, which is the enemy of timidity, that we can acquire serenity, the most enviable of all gifts, because it leads us near to Happiness by making it possible for us to discern Beauty sleeping in every thing.